D1534773

The Japanese Factory

The Japanese Factory

James [C.] Abegglen

ARNO PRESS
A New York Times Company
New York • 1979

Editorial Supervision: DIETRICH SNELL

Reprint edition 1979 by Arno Press Inc.

Copyright © 1958 by The Massachusetts Institute
of Technology
Reprinted by permission of The Free Press,
Division of Macmillan Publishing Co. Inc.
Reprinted from a copy in the State Library of Pennsylvania

PERENNIAL WORKS IN SOCIOLOGY
ISBN for complete set: 0-405-12081-8
See last pages of this volume for titles.

Manufactured in the United States of America

Library of Congress Cataloging in Publication Data

Abegglen, James C
    The Japanese factory.

    (Perennial works in sociology)
    Reprint of the 1958 ed. published by the
Free Press, Glencoe, Ill.
    1. Factory system--Japan. 2. Industrial
relations--Japan. I. Title. II. Series.
[HD2356.J3A6 1979]   338.6'5'0952   79-6982
ISBN 0-405-12082-6

THE JAPANESE FACTORY

Errata

The author's name on the cover and title page should read James C. Abegglen.

The titles of Chapters 7 and 8 have been transposed in the text.

The Center for International Studies
MASSACHUSETTS INSTITUTE OF TECHNOLOGY

The Japanese Factory

ASPECTS OF ITS SOCIAL ORGANIZATION

by James G. Abegglen

The Free Press, Glencoe, Illinois

CONTENTS

FOREWORD

The rate of economic growth of Japan between 1870 and the present has been higher than that of almost any other country in the world. As Dr. Abegglen's study shows, the social structure of Japanese factories is inconsistent with practices which Americans believe basic to the efficient conduct of a business concern. Indeed, if judged from the viewpoint of the American business executive, Japanese personnel principles and relationships are inefficient.

Yet they are efficient—highly efficient. The proof of the pudding is in the eating.

The moral is that the interpersonal relationships which will be effective in economic activity in a given country depend on the country's culture. Principles of business administration are not absolute; they are relative to the culture of the society.

This fact has come to be realized by most specialists in industrial relations. It is less clearly realized by many experts in business administration, both academic and practical, and it is by no means fully recognized by all students of the economic development of low-income countries.

Dr. Abegglen's clear and effective presentation of the social relationships within Japanese factories may be read with profit by all of these groups of individuals. I believe his book will be of significance both for the theory of business management and for the theory of economic development.

The Center for International Studies is currently engaged in research into the motivations that lead to economic growth. Believing that the circumstances which explain economic growth are not only economic but also lie in personality structure and in social relations, the Center is conducting empirical studies of the circumstances which have motivated groups of men in erstwhile "traditional" societies to enter effectively into economic development. Although it was done under a Ford Foundation grant before he joined the Center's staff for the year 1956–1957, Dr. Abegglen's work in Japan is closely related to these studies. The Center is sponsoring publication of this monograph because of its relationship to our "motivations project" and because of the importance of Dr. Abegglen's findings.

Everett E. Hagen

Director, Motivations Project

September 1957

PREFACE

The observations and data reported here are the result of more than a year's study in Japan, a second visit to that country. My primary purpose during this period of residence was to make a general study of Japan and the Japanese language. Within these limits of time and purpose an effort was made to gain a range of information on Japanese factories, especially the ways in which the people who make up these industrial groups come together and organize themselves for industrial production.

In this study a deliberate emphasis was placed on the large factory. First, since it represents an extreme in economic development, it was hoped that possible future trends would be indicated. Second, concentration on the large units seemed justified in terms of their central and dominating role in the manufacturing sectors in which they appear. In Japan large plants, defined as those employing more than 1,000 persons, are estimated to produce only some 15 per cent of the national product, but their role and influence in the economy are such as to make these proportions deceptive, for each has a most intimate relationship with a number of small plants. Third, in view of the general trend of Asian economic development it is probable that heavy industry, and consequently large factory units, will play an increasingly large role in the

Japanese economy. For these reasons this report, except where otherwise noted, is phrased in terms of the large Japanese factory.

A total of 19 large factories and 34 small factories was observed. The large factories employed from 2,000 to 8,000 persons and were major Japanese producers in their fields. They represented the following types of operations: chemicals (2), steel (2), aluminum (1), machinery (2), electrical equipment (2), radio communications equipment (1), mining (2), wire and cable manufacture (2), shipbuilding (2), and textiles (3). Most of the smaller factories were textile-producing units, but small chemical, electrical equipment, and metals-processing plants were also observed. Here "small" means factories employing up to 200 persons, for the most part 8 to 20 persons. Although the factory sites do not represent a systematic selection of units, the range and number and the extensive areas of congruence of methods and organization noted among the factories studied encourages the view that they do indeed represent the clear central style of organization in large Japanese industry.

The installations visited were on three of the four main islands of Japan—Honshu, Shikoku, and Hokkaido. The time spent at each site varied greatly. The large factories in the Tokyo and Osaka areas were revisited; those located some distance from Tokyo were visited for single periods of up to five days, largely with no opportunity for re-observation. Most of the smaller units were seen for brief periods. With the exception of a group of small textile plants near Tokyo, which were revisited periodically over several months, a typical visit consisted of several hours of interviewing and observing. These listings of sites and of time do not, of course, include work in the main offices of the large companies.

In the larger factories the customary procedures involved an initial meeting with a senior official of the company, usually the chief of the personnel department (since the area of study was most closely related to personnel). Next there was a tour of the firm's factory in as much detail as desired, generally in the company of a production specialist. Subsequently, there were arranged interviews with a number of persons, including the plant manager, union representatives, members of the personnel department, and production supervisors, as well as meetings with foremen and workers. It should be added that the cooperation extended was extraordinary, with a considerable initiative taken by management to suggest and arrange meetings and interviews. In addition, such data as were available were readily provided as questions came up on wages, welfare programs, work force, and the like, and in some instances additional data were collected at no little trouble by the company. As a consequence of this cooperation, in addition to interviews, observations, and meetings with supervisors, quite unexpected opportunities were made available to learn more about the people in Japanese factories.

Besides the planned and unplanned occasions, interviews, and observations, an advantage was gained from the Japanese custom of providing an evening's entertainment for business guests. These evenings, generally with a top executive and members of his staff, were of great help in learning more about the Japanese businessman and his firm.

In studying the factories, use was also made of formal questionnaires. Japanese management is quite interested in learning more about company employees, owing in part to the distance socially between worker and manager in the company. Unfortunately, few survey and attitude testing techniques have been developed in academic Japan and, with the limited relations between industry and the universities in Japan, even these have been little used. Perhaps as a result of these factors, management in most plants was quite willing to assist in the collection of special data.

It is important to note here too the role of the investigator as it was defined in this study. Some difficulty was anticipated and little advice was available on the probable reactions of Japanese firms to observers from abroad. It should be quickly added that no substantial difficulties were in fact encountered, and that, on the contrary, the hospitality, generosity, and interest shown exceeded fondest hopes. This positive and helpful reaction may have been due to two factors. First, letters of introduction were obtained from American businessmen who have con-tinued contact with Japanese firms and businessmen. These identified the bearer as competent in the study of business organizations, provided a basis for a more personal relationship, and were implicitly credentials for acceptance in the business community from businessmen. Further, the investigator had no formal affiliation with a Japanese university, a point which was frequently questioned. Although the respect accorded the scholar in Japanese society is high indeed compared with the United States, confidence and trust of businessmen in Japanese academicians is more qualified. It was clearly an advantage, however, to be able to offer my academic credentials (Ford Foundation Fellow and Research Associate of the University of Chicago) and yet not be associated with a particular Japanese university. The investigator's role then was essen-tially that of an outsider, but of a qualified and friendly outsider. In this kind of study it seemed to be a useful role.

Quite apart from the limitations of this study in terms of sampling or of methods employed, some of its additional limits need to be noted. The background and frame of reference are those of factory organiza-tion in the United States. Since the United States stands at the other extreme from the Japanese factory in many aspects of industrial organization, a Japanese or a European observer would have attended more closely to factors which were neglected in this study. Similarly, the fact that the values of the investigator are those of an American was a factor in the study. Although it is incumbent on the observer to make every effort to recognize and reassess views and conclusions derived narrowly from his own background and beliefs, such effort will seldom be entirely successful in any study of human relationships. More concretely, in contrast to the United States there was no opportunity in Japan to work in a factory and experience at first hand the workings of the organization. Indeed, it would be difficult for a Japanese student to arrange to work at a lathe or drill press in a Japanese factory.

Still another limitation of this study was that most difficult of all hazards in studying Japan—the language. In early plant visits it was necessary to rely almost entirely on an interpreter provided by the company. By the end of the term of study, visits were made without interpreters, but at no point was real fluency achieved in either speech or reading.

Despite these limitations, warrant for this report on the Japanese factory is derived from the importance of the subject and the absence of firsthand and systematic information on the subject for persons working on problems of industrialization in non-Western countries. As an industrialized non-Western nation, Japan occupies a unique position in Asia. How industrialization was effected, how industry is carried on, and its effects on social organization in Japan—all are relevant to the problems of industrialization in other non-Western countries.

James C. Abegglen

Cambridge, Massachusetts
September 1957

ACKNOWLEDGMENTS

The thoughtful hospitality and assistance of many people made residence in Japan most pleasant and aided greatly in learning about Japanese industry. To these generous hosts and able teachers I offer deep thanks and my regrets for my inability to more adequately acknowledge their kindnesses. Special acknowledgment must be paid Asano Michiko, William Flanley, Hachiya Saburo, Kimura Yutaake, Kitagawa Kazue, Kuwamura Ken, Nabeshima Tsunatoshi, Takashima Hisao, Tsujimoto Kataharu, Howard Van Zandt, and Yamada Junichiro.

I am obliged to W. Lloyd Warner and Burleigh B. Gardner for instruction in the role of industrial organizations in social systems, and to Dr. Gardner and William H. Harrison, Jr. for their supervision of my work in American factories.

The support of Everett E. Hagen contributed greatly to the preparation and publication of this report. Valuable comments and suggestions were provided by Allan B. Cole, John D. Donoghue, Alexander Eckstein, Dr. Hagen, Komiya Ryotaru, Solomon B. Levine, and Tsura Shigeto. The study was made under a fellowship granted by The Ford Foundation; the conclusions and views are those of the author and not necessarily those of The Ford Foundation.

James C. Abegglen

1

INDUSTRY IN ASIA: THE CASE OF JAPAN

The present concern about the entire problem of industrialization has been compelled by the massive confrontation of the world's two great power centers. This confrontation is now taking place in the economic and industrial spheres, and the lives of most of the people of the world will be shaped irrevocably by the choice made in economic development between these power centers or some alternative approach to industrialization.

The choices of the route to industrialization cannot appear attractive to uncommitted nations. There is the Western alternative, industrialization arising out of a matrix including colonial exploitation, religious justification, and private, if not free, enterprise, a rapid but not meteoric change extending over some two centuries, wasteful of both time and resources. The Soviet alternative, posed again by China, affords the maximum of rapidity, the minimum use of external resources in capital, equipment, and personnel, and a surety of success from the very price paid—the terrible destructiveness of private and personal choice, initiative, and freedom.

To the Asian or African these must seem dubious alternatives indeed. In terms of the preservation of the values and ideals precious in his present "underdeveloped" world, the outcomes might well appear mutually distasteful. From the one direction there is a welter of commercialism, restlessness, confusion, and competition; from the other a monolithic and brutal orderliness—monochromatic, intemperate, and unrelaxing. Both alternatives threaten the erosion or destruction of his religion, his family system, and the tastes, habits, and even dress and speech produced over millennia. These areas are not "under-developed." They have developed fully but in a direction different from that which events now compel. There is little choice about the fact of change. The change will come and is now in process; the mode and the direction of change pose these rude alternatives.

It is at this point that Japan becomes of special interest. Japan is the single third party present now on the scene, a non-Western nation that might properly be described as industrial, which for all its industry remains clearly and consistently Asian. Japan has changed greatly in the century since it re-entered the world; it has incorporated new ideas, adapted its older institutions, and accommodated to alien and often distasteful modes. Still it remains true that Japan cannot be described in the terms used in describing a nation of the West. It is not simply a re-location of the arts, family system, social relations, or habits of thought that have come to be associated with industrialization throughout Europe and America. In some manner this enormous change in economic activity has been taken into an on-going culture and made into what might prove to be still another approach.

The unique experience of Japan as a non-Western industrialized nation poses an exceptional opportunity for those interested in the process of industrialization in other Asian nations. There is raised first of all a question, outside the scope of this report, as to how this process took place, a historical question concerning the causes and sources of this change. Another question, and the central question of this study, is the outcome of the process of industrialization in Japan. There is a marked tendency to view industrialization in terms of particular Western experiences—the Protestant ethic as a source of motivation, a trend to impersonalization of social interaction, the development of a rational world view by Western man. The question presents itself then as to how Western technology, modern industrial technology, may be fitted into a non-Western context with a different social inheritance. What kinds of adjustments must take place to fit this technology and the local peoples into an effective industrial unit?

These statements do not say or imply that Japan will furnish a case study from which may be predicted the course of industrialization in Indonesia, Burma, and India. Whatever the temptation to speak generally of Asia, this kind of generalization cannot be made from one to another of such enormously diverse cultures and peoples. The experience of Japan does provide, however, one test of the limits of adaptation, a measure of the kinds of alternatives to the technology-human relations interaction seen in the West which can be useful in attempting to estimate the range of adaptations and adjustments possible or necessary in introducing a technology which is the product of one kind of culture into another culture.

Apart from the several scientific questions implicit in this issue, there are some immediate and practical problems involved. As the West in general, and the United States in particular, embarks on programs to aid the economic development of non-Western nations, our ambassadors and envoys are drawn in large numbers from the ranks of engineers and businessmen, groups whose experience is usually confined to a single nation. Such personnel are clearly necessary and appropriate for the job to be done. Unfortunately, it seems true that ethnocentrism is particularly strong in the area of technological and business procedures. Thus there is a tendency to assume that since, let us say, job evaluation is useful and effective in American industry, it will be similarly useful and effective, even essential, in the industrial plants of Indonesia. If time study is a prerequisite to the effective use of machines in a plant in Ohio, the thinking goes, it must also be introduced into the organization of a plant in Shikoku. Perhaps these techniques should be used, but these industrial methods assume a great deal about the setting and people and involve problems of which the consultant or advisor might well be totally unaware. Although these are bread-and-butter problems, they illustrate a more general trend of thought about larger issues of organization and management. Furthermore, these small issues themselves can, and on occasion do, become major factors in the success or failure of American attempts to aid industrialization in different cultures. The study of industrialization in Japan may make possible a closer examination of some of the limits of these procedures and of the adaptation in the Western production system that may be necessary.

This, then, is the broad context in which this study of Japanese industrial organization should be viewed. In order to bring about more effectively the orderly and rapid economic development of other nations and to make this technology fit more effectively into the on-going patterns of social relations in non-Western nations, there is an urgent need for a further understanding of the outcomes of the introduction of modern industrial technology into cultures markedly different from our own. From the study of the outcomes of the Japanese experience, the methods employed in the social organization of Japanese factories, and the problems posed at present in Japanese industry by the lack of fit between technology and social custom, an approach to economic development in Asia might better be conceived.

A further objective of the study reported here was to add to the understanding of modern Japan through the detailed examination of a limited problem. Leaving aside descriptions of Japan by self-exiled romantics and the results of war-fevered attention, a very considerable part of the studies of Japan move on a quite general level. Attention to Japan's history and art has been substantial; but in speaking of modern Japan there is a distressing frequency of sentences beginning, "The Japanese are. . . . ," which treat the nation and its people as a compact and homogeneous unit with little or no note of the diversity and complexity of this modern nation. Most general is the view of Japan as a nation of fishing villages and farming hamlets, isolated communities, and ancient festivals. Although these elements are present in modern Japan, to understand the nation they must be seen in focus with Japan's sprawling, ugly cities, jammed with people, interlaced by high-speed transportation, smoky and noisy, and filled with the clamor and tension of commerce and industry.

There is a need for particularistic studies, aimed at the more detailed examination of problem areas which will spell out the full scope of diversity and complexity, to provide a more balanced view of Japan. It is to this end that studies of the Japanese factory might contribute. Despite the importance of Japanese industry in world economic affairs and the constant interaction, both friendly and competitive, between Western and Japanese enterprises, such studies are few in number. The importance of the topic, no less than the paucity of specific information, encouraged this report on some aspects of Japanese factories.

The study of the social organization of Japanese industry is thus taken to derive its relevance, first, from the intrinsic interest and importance of Japanese industry in the understanding of Japan and, second, from the possible implications of the Japanese experience and outcomes in industrialization for economic development of other non-Western countries. It might be hoped that a further by-product of such studies would be a contribution to the understanding of our own industrial organizations. Although the experimental methods as commonly conceived cannot usually be applied to persons or cultures, it is possible to approximate an experimental comparison of two cultures which will cast light on the underlying social dynamics of both cultures. The ethnocentrism referred to earlier has no doubt interfered with effective understanding of our own industrialization. Comparison with a nation like Japan may well further understanding of the United States.

Within this general framework of goals this study had as its objective a more particular problem. The emphasis on economic development of nonindustrial societies has led to a considerable interest in the history of the Japanese transition to industrialization. Analyses of the process of industrialization and the causes of economic development in Japan proceed, generally, on the assumption that the outcome of industrialization in that country has been, in terms of social organization and interpersonal relations, largely identical with the outcomes of industrialization in the West.

For example, a recent discussion of the social basis for Japan's rapid industrialization described as the outcome of the process the appearance of "an entirely different sort of social relationship than had been common in either China or Japan," and continues, "In the sphere of relationships industrialization carried with it an emphasis hitherto unequaled in social history on what the sociologists speak of as highly rational, highly universalistic, and highly functionally specific relationships."[1] The analysis of industrialization in Japan seems generally to proceed on the assumption that there occurred a transition from an earlier system of interpersonal relationships to this pattern of interpersonal relationships, a transition to the kind of interactions between people observed to be characteristic of Western societies under conditions of industrialization.

The assumption that the results of industrialization in Japan have paralleled and been similar to those witnessed in the West not only underlies much of the academic analysis of the nature of the Japanese experience in the transition to an industrial economy but also is implicit in much of the effort to increase productivity in the Japanese factory. Owing in part to this assumption, methods and machines useful in British and American production are introduced into the Japanese factory with little attention to their appropriateness for what may be a mark - edly different organizational context. The assumption of similarity in organizational systems and in relationships in industry is in error. As a consequence, some of the analyses of the causes of Japan's industrialization as well as much of the effort to increase Japanese production do not achieve their purpose.

The close relationship between the organization of the total society and the organization of its industry has been demonstrated by considerable research in recent decades.[2] Given this evidence, it might be

[1] Marion J. Levy, Jr., "Contrasting Factors in the Modernization of China and Japan," in Economic Growth: Brazil, India, Japan, Simon Kuznets, Wilbert E. Moore, and Joseph J. Spengler, Eds. (Durham: Duke University Press, 1955).

[2] Important early contributions to this now substantial literature include Elton Mayo, The Human Problems of an Industrial Civilization (New York: The Macmillan Company, 1933), and F. J. Roethlisberger and W. J. Dickson, Manage-

argued that, as a result of the differences between Japan and the West in pre-industrial and present social organization, the present organization of the factory would differ in systematic ways in the two types of societies. Thus the social outcomes of technological change would not fit the pattern anticipated from a projection of the Western outcomes onto Japanese society. Again, the view that the Meiji Restoration and surrounding events constituted a basic and thoroughgoing revolution in Japanese society has been modified by indications that the changes in Japan after the 1860's grew out of earlier trends, impluses, and events and that the element of social discontinuity has been overstated in describing these eventful decades.[3] Thus it might be argued that, whatever form industrial organization has taken in Japan, as an outgrowth of earlier forms of social organization, it would be systematically different from the Western model.

This report was shaped by the fact that the question of the degree of resemblance between industrial organization in the West and in Japan has been but little explored. This statement is especially true of the large business firm, on which no literature is now available in English for the interested observer; small firms as well have been reported on but little.[4] Indeed, with the lack of a tradition of and in-

---

ment and the Worker (Cambridge: Harvard University Press, 1939), as well as the work of W. Lloyd Warner, William A. Whyte, and others.

[3] See, especially, George B. Sansom, The Western World and Japan: A Study in the Interaction of European and Asiatic Cultures (New York: Alfred A. Knopf, 1950), and Donald Keene, The Japanese Discovery of Europe: Honda Toshiaki and Other Discoverers, 1720-1798. (London: Routledge and Kegan Paul, Ltd., 1952).

[4] Two recent papers discussing the small factory in Japan are John Pelzel, "The Small Industrialist in Japan," Explorations in Entrepreneurial History, Vol. 7 (December 1954), and Lawrence Olson, "A Japanese Small Industry: A letter from Kyoto," Explorations in Entrepreneurial History, Vol. 8 (April 1956).

terest in empirical field studies in Japanese social science, especially in the fields of sociology and psychology, there is little relevant information available in Japanese literature.[5] The research conducted for this report was therefore exploratory in nature. For this reason and because the area of study was a broad and complex one and an intimate grasp of the setting, Japan, is not readily achieved by the external observer, this report is in no way complete or final. Rather, it is an attempt, on the basis of limited observation, to set out the broad outlines of the organization of the Japanese factory.

It will be the burden of this report to show that, whatever their similarities in technology and external appearance, the American and Japanese factory organizations differ in important ways. Examining in turn the nature of the basic relationship between employee and firm, the recruitment of personnel by the company, and the systems of rewards employed in the factory, consistent differences will be seen, differences which have immediate and important effects on the kind of technology and management methods that can be used in the organization. Further, it will be seen that within the organization the extent and nature of the involvement of the firm in the life of the worker are based on different assumptions as to the nature of the work relationship.

[5]Commenting on this field, a leading Japanese sociologist remarked, "Research on industrial relations and union problems in our country has been deficient in close analyses of human relations in organizations and in unions. No small part [of such studies] are very general discussions . . . critical 'theories' which dispense with detailed investigation, various legal discussions, arguments for institutional reform, and ideological controversies. Summing up, these comments will indicate the low level of social science in this country. For these reasons we feel very strongly the necessity of promoting in this country detailed, close researches on issues in human relations." Odaka Kunio, Sangyo ni okeru Ningen Kankei no Kagaku (Science of Human Relations in Industry) (Tokyo: Yuhikaku Kabushiki Kaisha, 1953), p. 178.

In short, in the critical areas of interpersonal relations and group interaction, in the definition of the nature of the relationship between worker and company, and in the way in which skills and energies are mobilized and directed in the group, the Japanese factory is a variant of industrialization from the American factory. These variations may be seen as deriving essentially from the differences between the broader social systems of the United States and Japan. An understanding of these variations is essential to an understanding of Japanese industry and, more important, to working with and effectively assisting in the further development of Japanese industry. From the Japanese experience, too, relevant clues may be gained as to the kinds of problems that may be encountered with the introduction of industrial technology into other non-Western nations.

2

THE CRITICAL DIFFERENCE: A LIFETIME COMMITMENT

When comparing the social organization of the factory in Japan and the United States one difference is immediately noted and continues to dominate and represent much of the total difference between the two systems. At whatever level of organization in the Japanese factory, the worker commits himself on entrance to the company for the remainder of his working career. The company will not discharge him even temporarily except in the most extreme circumstances. He will not quit the company for industrial employment elsewhere. He is a member of the company in a way resembling that in which persons are members of families, fraternal organizations, and other intimate and personal groups in the United States.

This rule of a lifetime commitment is truly proved by its rare exceptions, and the permanent relationship between employee and firm imposes obligations and responsibilities on both the factory and the worker of a different order than that on which personnel practices and worker-company relationships in the United States are built. The difference between the two systems is not, of course, absolute, but one of degree. Reluctance on the part of the worker to quit and on the part of the firm to fire him are constant factors in the American relationship; the Japanese firm will discharge employees, and employees do occasionally quit.

The magnitude of the difference is very great, however, and its consequences and implications will be seen repeatedly throughout this description of the large Japanese factory.

To illustrate the Japanese practice the labor exit rates of two large firms for several years will be examined. The first is an electrical equipment manufacturing firm in the Osaka area. The company employs some 4,350 persons, of whom five or six are fired each year, or about one per thousand. These discharges are for reason of extreme behavior— e.g., a man who had not been in the plant for some weeks, following a series of similar absentee periods, or a worker accused of habitual and substantial thievery of company property—that is, the breach of conduct is so considerable as to allow no alternative to discharge.

As to labor exits for reasons other than discharge, the annual rate for the 5-year period 1949-1953 was 83 out of 3,337 men and 109 of a total of 1,014 women, or a labor departure rate of between 2 and 3 per cent for men and about 10 per cent for women. Of the men, about two-fifths had reached retirement age; the remainder left the company for reasons of health or, more often, to return to the family farm after the death of a father or brother. (Since 1953 the exit rate for male employees in this firm has actually dropped and in 1956 was at the rate of 1.7 per cent.) Among the women, since very few continue in the company's employ until their retirement age of 50 years, marriage, not age, accounted for almost all of the exits. Although there is no absolute sanction against married women working, in this company, as in all others, both company pressure and social custom almost demand that a married woman leave the job market.

It must be noted here that temporary layoffs because of lack of work do not take place in this or any other firm encountered in the course of this study. The company has full responsibility for the continued salary of all its employees for the duration of their employment, which is usually the full term of the working career. It is no wonder then that workers are often termed "permanent" or "eternal" employees.[1]

This firm is in no way exceptional in the exit rate of its employees. The highest annual rate of exit encountered in the large factories studied was in a textile plant in Shikoku, employing about 3,500 workers. Here the annual rate of exit for men over the five-year period 1951-1955 was 3.6 per cent. This comparatively high percentage was caused by the plant's rural location, the rate of return to rural occupations being somewhat higher than usual. The exit rate for women was about 14 per cent annually, again somewhat higher than in the urban plant.

These percentages include both management personnel and workers. An example of the exit rate of top management personnel taken alone is provided by the situation in a Tokyo firm. Top management was composed of 14 men, only 6 of whom had entered the firm immediately on completion of their schooling. At first sight this figure appeared to be a sharp departure from the general rule cited above, but closer examination proved it to be no exception. The firm was a member of one of the major prewar zaibatsu or cartel groups. Of the 8 men whose careers

---

[1] The description of job relations given here is held to describe the general rule in the large factories of Japan. In a few types of industries, notably in construction and shipbuilding, worker recruitment and intraplant relations differ somewhat from those described in this report. Also, in the smaller and specialized shops of the large cities (e.g., in printing), movement of a worker from one to another job is more common and accepted. In the textile industry, where the proportion of female employees is high, data on the rate of exit of female workers provides an apparent exception to the above rules. Since women are expected and encouraged to marry, even assisted in marriage, after five to seven years of employment and must leave the company at the time of marriage, the rate of employee exit is high, which does not, however, alter the nature of the commitment of worker and company through the employment period.

were seemingly spent in large part outside this company, 5 had come to the company from the <u>zaibatsu</u> bank and one from the trading company.[2] In short, both top management and workers stand in the same lifetime relationship to the company. The exceptions in no way negate the rule.

Viewing the over-all social organization of the Japanese factory, it is clear that the lasting commitment of employee and employer, by which the employer will not discharge or lay off the worker and the worker will not leave the company's employ, is the result of and a striking example of a major difference between Western and Japanese job relationships. The Western relationship is more nearly "contractual." Both parties to the contract note that under certain conditions not necessarily related to the performance of his job the worker will be free to leave the company's employ and the company will be free to ask him to leave. He may be offered by another company a higher position, more pay or leisure, more opportunity for advancement, or a better location. He may within specified rules terminate the relationship and, more important, if he does so no particular stigma attaches to his leaving. On the contrary, he may well be seen as a more intelligent, more ambitious, more able person for having found a better position. In the same manner, the company, while more limited in its discretion, may for reasons usually having to do with its financial position terminate the relationship.

A rather high rate of movement from job to job and company to company characterizes both American workers and executive personnel. Generally, a high rate of mobility is considered desirable in American

[2] The remaining two apparent exceptions were of special interest in terms of the interrelations of business and politics in Japan. One of these men did not join the firm until he was 62 years of age; he had been a judge in an important court in the Japanese judicial system. The other, who entered the company at the age of 61, was and is a member of the Diet's majority party. He was also the only nonuniversity graduate among the top management group.

business. Such terms as "the free play of the labor market" and "cross-fertilization of management" convey the belief that the limited job commitment and limited worker-firm relationship are usually advantageous so long as the rate of movement does not interfere with the continued presence of trained personnel.

Although the system of job relationships employed in Japan might be supported by the argument that it ensures the continued use of company-trained personnel, the rationale presented by Japanese management ordinarily emphasizes other points. Its policy toward dismissals and lay-offs is usually explained in terms of larger national issues and problems. The most frequent justification offered is that Japan is a poor country and an overpopulated one, a country where jobs are scarce and employment difficult. Laid-off or dismissed workers will simply starve, the argument goes, because they will be able to find no other work. For the employees' sakes, therefore, the company must ensure continued salaries at all times. This approach to employment is also justified in terms of the national welfare. Since jobs are scarce and the population large, it is the duty of management to maximize the number of positions in the plant and refrain from reducing the work force. In the interest of the national economy management has a duty to employ as many people as possible at all times.

These arguments on the part of Japanese management to justify its personnel policy are worth fairly close attention. They are revealing both of management thinking in Japan and of the broader underlying interpersonal relations in the factory. First of all, Japanese management at all levels is prone to think in large national terms and is quite conscious of the interaction between business policy and national welfare. This concern for the national well-being is no doubt a consequence both of the historical intimacy of government and business in Japan and of the high consciousness of the impact of business policy on national welfare in a nation so dependent on import-export exchange for its survival.

The argument that Japan is a poor country has become a national cliché. It is applied to virtually all inconveniences and discomforts in Japan, with, on occasion, no apparent connection between the problem and the announced poverty. In relation to employment practices, it might well be argued that the national economy would be aided by an increased efficiency in factory output resulting from increased labor mobility and a responsiveness of the work force to the workings of supply-demand factors. The argument justifying permanent employment in terms of national well-being might be seen most accurately as a rationalization of a system rather than as an explanation of a real cause of the system of job relations.

In addition to the argument concerning national economic welfare, another aspect of the explanation by Japanese management of the factory-worker relationship should be noted. Japanese management argues that laid-off or discharged workers will face financial disaster and the company therefore must not lay off and may fire workers only in cases of extreme provocation. It is true that a worker of whatever competence is hard put to find new employment if it is known (and his age will indicate) that he has been fired or laid off from a job. This becomes a circular problem, however. Since, under the present system, layoff means incompetence of the most drastic sort, it is not surprising that a layoff or discharge on a man's work record is taken automatically to mean that he is not suitable for further employment.[3] The system is in this way self-

[3] In this connection it is interesting to note the complaints of American businessmen in Japan that they are not able to hire first-rate Japanese college graduates. The threat of a limited work period and the subsequent difficulties in re-estab-

reinforcing. Again the argument is more a rationalization of the existing system than a convincing analysis of the reasons for the permanent
employer-employee relationship.

In a purely economic definition of employment terms, where the
financial success of the factory is the overriding goal of management's
policy, the national well-being and workers' welfare would be secondary considerations in much policy formation. Underlying the specific
points made in support of the Japanese policy, and quite aside from
the validity of these points, is the tacit recognition by management
that the relationship between the company and the worker is not simply a function of the economic convenience of the two parties. The
worker, whether laborer or manager, may not at his convenience leave
the company for another position. He is bound, despite potential economic advantage, to remain in the company's employ. The company,
for its part, must not dismiss the worker to serve its own financial ends.
Loyalty to the group and an interchange of responsibilities—a system
of shared obligation—take the place of the economic basis of employment of worker by the firm.

The area of mutual interchange of responsibility and obligation
goes considerably beyond the regulations and practices governing employment and dismissal. Taking this one factor alone, however, wide-
ranging and serious consequences of this permanent kind of job relationship may be mentioned.

In the Japanese factory at the present time it is commonly noted
and readily admitted that there is almost always a surplus of labor over
the number required to maintain the level of production. By American

---

lishing themselves in the Japanese business world make the Western firms an
insecure job avenue for these young men.

factory standards there is an astonishing proliferation of make-work jobs, jobs often of a menial sort—tea servers, sweepers, messengers, doorkeepers, and the like—which could be substantially and easily reduced in numbers, as well as a great deal of inefficient use of time and energy in productive jobs.

Using American standards it is not possible to compare directly the productivity of Japanese and American factories. For example, since the greater part of unit cost in American production is usually assumed to be labor costs, it is mandatory to maximize the use of machine processes in production. The reverse is true in Japan, where labor costs are such that the machine is the luxury and the laborer the lower-cost productive unit. However, the fact remains that even within the Japanese system of production the typical factory has a substantial surplus of workers, which is a direct result of the inability of management to lay off or dismiss workers.

There are further consequences of this labor immobility which affect seriously the economic well-being of the factory and the nation. They are felt in two particular aspects of the economy. The first is that of technological change. Clearly, where a surplus of laborers presently exists there is a much reduced incentive to introduce new methods or machinery into production. The result is to enhance a conservative attitude toward change which is already fairly strong in the thinking of factory management. However, it is not possible for management to totally resist technological change. Several factors make for an inexorable shift toward increasingly mechanized, labor-saving production methods and an exacerbation of the problem of labor surplus. One of these is, of course, the output of new products, products obtained by purchase of foreign patents or, less often, through local development. The new product is adopted along with the more mechanized productive system devised at the time the product was developed in, say, Germany or the United States. As a consequence, comparable output of this product with the one it replaces is ordinarily less demanding of labor.

Another and more important factor in technological change, which leads to an increasingly severe labor problem, is the pressure felt by Japanese management to use new methods and new machines. Japanese management looks now, as in the early development of Japanese industry, to foreign and, at present, chiefly American, sources for ideas and techniques. These vary from particular engineering methods to those of general management. Insofar as new technology is introduced, however, it has nearly always had the effect of exacerbating the already present problem of labor surplus in the factory. It should be noted that this is a different kind of problem from that caused by the introduction of automation, for example, in an American firm. In the United States the problem might become a community or national one of a total surplus of labor; in Japan the labor surplus would present a serious problem for the management of the particular factory which introduced the change.

The second category of difficulty created by the worker-firm relationship in Japan has to do with the impact of sudden economic change on the factory. Here an example might be taken from recent history. In the early days of the postwar American occupation of Japan, a considerable economic inflation took place. On the recommendation of a committee of American financial advisors the Japanese government undertook in 1949 a rather sudden and considerable change in policy. One result was a drop in economic activity, known to Japanese businessmen as the "Dodge depression" in commemoration of the head of the advisory group. The effects on many companies were little short of catastrophic. Apart from such firms as those in textiles, the products of which were in little demand during the war years, as a result of wartime expansion most large firms were committed to very large work forces. They had managed to carry these employees through the early postwar years, but the situation in 1949 became such that they simply could no longer do so. In a number of companies this depression became the occasion for a kind of drastic surgery unprecedented in company history, a surgery that came to be known as "rationalization." This step called for heroic measures, and their magnitude indicates the extreme difficulty management has in adapting to sudden shifts in economic tides.

In one company the work force, both management and labor, was reduced in eight months from 3,926 to 3,206 persons. About 600 workers and 125 staff members were "voluntarily retired." Although the term sounds ironic in the Japanese context, it appears that these were in fact voluntary retirements. Workers were offered their normal full retirement allowance plus a special allowance, the total payment in most cases amounting to about 500,000 yen. Noting that the average monthly wage payment in this plant in 1949 was about 10,000 yen it will be seen that the inducement to retire was substantial—and enormously costly to management. Those who retired were largely older persons nearing normal retirement, who took advantage of the special allowance, and women who used the sum as a substantial addition to their dowries. In all, 15 per cent of the firm's laborers left, 9 per cent of the men and 32 per cent of the women; and 9 per cent of the staff retired, 5 per cent of the men and 21 per cent of the women. These

were all voluntary retirements, and the special high cost is a measure
of the great difficulties involved in adjusting the size of the work force
in a Japanese factory.

This drastic move brought with it, it might be noted, two problems
for the future which are currently worrying management. By lowering
the average age of the work force, recent retirements have been few
in number and will suddenly become considerable in the not-too-distant
future. More awkward, since it was difficult to induce staff personnel
to retire, a number of companies now have a large surplus of staff and
managerial personnel, with resulting depressing effects on promotion
rate, morale, and job efficiency.

The "Dodge depression" and its effect on this one plant may serve
to make the point that, whatever the advantages of a continuing obligation on the part of the worker and firm to remain in relationship, it
is extremely difficult to achieve any measure of flexibility of work
force within the Japanese system. The 1949 economic crisis did not
affect all plants and firms to the same extent; this "rationalization"
was by no means universal. However, all Japanese factories have a
similar set of problems arising from the same causes, even those firms
which have shown an increase in plant size or total business.

A minor example of the difficulties arising out of worker immobility
in an expanding firm might be taken from the experience of a large
metals-processing firm. This company has plants in several parts of
Japan, and a rather new installation is located in south-central Honshu.
To attempt to reduce somewhat the oversupply of labor in other plants,
an effort was made to staff the newer plant, as its production increased,
with workers from other plants. This transfer had taken place from one
of the plants studied. Of the 40 men assigned and moved to the new

location, 2 had committed suicide within two weeks. Although the firm did not yet have enough information to be sure of the causes, there was a generally held view that the suicides were the result of the men's inability both to deal with the fact of being transferred and to adjust to the new situation. Although an extreme case, this example suggests that the immobility of Japanese labor is not merely an economic problem.

Alternatives to the rigidity of the work force are offered by two aspects of present-day Japanese factory organization that can serve as buffers against the consequences of economic and technological change. The most direct practice is the utilization of "temporary" employees. The over-all rule discussed until now applies to the category of employees referred to as "permanent" or "regular," including all staff employees and the great majority of laborers. However, most plants have a group of employees toward whom they do not have the same measure of responsibility, and who do not participate in the relationship previously described. The number of these employees varies with the work demands in the plant, the maximum observed being about 10 per cent of the total laboring force. Legally these temporary employees can be laid off after two months of employment. They are usually hired through the government employment offices and frequently represent agricultural labor surplus (persons of farm background are generally considered desirable employees). Previous factory experience or training is not necessary for their employment and they perform lower-level tasks, often at the lowest possible salary. Clearly this system of supplementary labor recruitment cannot replace in any substantial degree the primary system, but it does provide some measure of adaptability and flexibility to the work force. It should be added that workers ordinarily do not move from the ranks of temporary to permanent employees in the same company.

Another aspect of the Japanese factory system that plays some part in the amelioration of the consequences of the worker–firm relationship is the considerable number of affiliated and subordinate companies attached to a large factory. Subcontracting, sometimes within the plant of the parent company, often takes place. To the extent that increases in output might be met through subcontracting rather than through an attempted increase in productivity of the parent firm, the problem of increasing the labor force to meet increased business would be displaced to the smaller company. In general, however, subcontracting is confined to peripheral processes and to particular items. Further, it is no less difficult for the small firm to lay off or fire than for the large firm; indeed, in many ways it is more difficult. The union may play some part in maintaining the no–lay–off rule and in ensuring its rigid adherence in the large firm, whereas the small plant will probably not be unionized. The personal relationship between employer and employee is strong in the small plant, however, and the rule of custom in the neighborhood or village in which the small plant is located is so effective that it is impossible, short of real bankruptcy, for most small factory owners to reduce their work force.

One further alternative for admitting some flexibility into the work force was reported, although it had not been resorted to for many years in any of the factories observed. In the event of a lack of work in the plant so complete as to preclude retaining the labor force, management has been able in the past to send workers home for a time. During this no–work period, the persons "laid off" continue to be employees of the company and are paid a salary of 60 per cent of their usual income. This pay, despite no work performed, continues until the workers are recalled or the company dissolves as an

organization. This device was resorted to during the depression of the
1930's and is not a factor in plant operations except in such an emer-
gency period.

One possible future consequence of this permanent employment system might be pointed out. Japan subsists on export, and its exports are
largely competitive with those of the most advanced technologies,
Germany, England, and the United States. Even in a nation where
labor cost is low compared to the cost of capital and equipment, there
is a limit to the extent to which low labor cost can be employed to
counterbalance a lesser rate of technological progress. Further, the
labor cost per unit of production in Japan is rising and is likely to continue to rise. It is at this future point of competitive disadvantage that
the full consequences of this rigidity of relationships within the factory
are likely to be felt. Again, one of the results of Japan's dependence
on exports is a particular sensitivity to changes in economic conditions
in other parts of the world. Here, also, a premium is placed on the
capacity to adapt quickly, to be able to maintain a considerable flexibility to meet changing market conditions. In these respects, whatever
the noneconomic advantages or disadvantages for the individuals from
the contrasting bases of job relationships in Japan and the West, in
terms of economic outcomes there appears to be a considerable potential for serious trouble in the future of the Japanese factory.

Since the immobility of the Japanese work force both within and
between factories has so considerable an effect on the present functioning and future prospects of Japanese industry, and since it offers a
clear contrast to the American practice, the problem has been examined
here first and in some detail. The full meaning of this kind of worker-
firm relationship, however, can be shown only in the wider context of

the social organization of the Japanese factory. This kind of commitment between employee and employer is closely interrelated with the system of recruitment, the system of motivation and reward, and, indeed, is a basic part of the entire Japanese factory organization. Although it is possible to discuss the single aspect of the immobility of Japanese in isolation from the whole fabric of worker-firm relations, it does not function in such isolation, and to change this one element would affect profoundly the entire system. Before concluding that this is a disadvantageous employment system it is first necessary to look at other elements of the factory organization to gauge the effects of a possible change in this one factor.

3

THE RECRUITMENT OF PERSONNEL

A system of organization in which membership is semi-permanent may be expected to attach considerable importance to the recruitment and selection of its personnel. Where the job relationship is a more limited one, contractual and subject to termination, errors in selection need not weigh heavily in the successful operation of the organization. Where the employer-employee relationship is virtually irreversible and the commitment is for the career of both parties, errors in selection of organization personnel can seldom be rectified and demand a considerable price in organizational efficiency.

The Japanese factory presents a rather contradictory picture in terms of procedures for the recruitment and selection of personnel. There is an elaborate selection system in effect in the larger firms. At the same time, the basis for the selection of personnel and the avenues of recruitment are very different from those in the United States. The general difference lies in a greater dependence in selection in Japan on certain recruiting and selecting processes inherent in the broader social system—e. g., the relationship between student and teacher in the universities—and on qualities of character and background not directly related to the work position. Less attention is given to those qualities of the individual and methods of selection—e.g., aptitude and personality tests—which function in isolation from the social system and are evaluated in terms of potential performance on a specific job.

The selection of personnel in a Japanese factory is related more closely to education than to any other consideration. Both the categories of employees selected and the methods used in contacting and screening future employees depend very much on the way in which the Japanese schools are organized and on the reputations and personnel of the schools.

The Japanese educational system at the present time follows the 6-3-3-4 year pattern in common use in the United States. Introduced by the Occupation authorities following the Second World War, the system is relatively new in Japan, and the people by no means unanimously support this system. Indeed, it appears likely that it will be modified in the future. However that may be, the present scheduling of education consists of six years of primary school, three of middle school, three of higher school, and four of college or university work.

The prewar system does not readily lend itself to a comparison with this American-style scheduling, since it was based on a European model. There were available specialized middle and higher schools providing occupational training in agriculture and industry for students who did not continue to a higher educational level. It is important to note, too, that graduation from the higher school of prewar Japan carried with it a level of accomplishment more nearly equivalent to graduation from an American junior college. Many problems, some of which will be apparent from the following discussion of factory recruitment, were created for Japan by the arbitrary and short-sighted imposition of a sharply different system of educational scheduling. However, since the newer system is that on which present recruitment methods are based, it will be largely in terms of this division of education that current recruitment practices will be described.

To provide a general indication of the nature of the relation between education and recruitment that exists in the Japanese factory, the figures in Table 1 present the position in the organizational scheme and the education of all managers and supervisors and a ten per cent sample of wage and salary workers in a large manufacturing plant.

Table 1

POSITION IN THE FACTORY AND
EDUCATIONAL BACKGROUND

	Educational Background		
Factory Position	Primary and Middle School (Per Cent)	Higher School (Per Cent)	College or University (Per Cent)
Wage worker, female	100	0	0
Wage worker, male	100	0	0
Salary worker, female	11	89	0
Salary worker, male	16	73	11
Second-level supervisors	1	46	53
First-level supervisors	0	16	84
Top management	0	10	90

It will be noted that all wage workers are persons who have received no more education than that required by law. No persons who have received more than the minimal education are in the wage-worker group. Only about 15 per cent of the salary workers, male and female, are less than high school graduates; and these, it should be added, are older persons, graduates of the former middle school. No female university graduates are employed in this particular plant. Three-fourths of the male salary workers are high school graduates, and the great majority of supervisors are college graduates. The sole member of top management not graduated from college was a graduate of the old-system higher school. The sharpness of differences by education between ranks is partially obscured in Table 1 by combining the old and new systems. For example, the importance of college for selection into the supervisory and management level is concealed by the presence of graduates of the old-system higher school, actually equivalent to some college, in the higher school category.

Table 1 serves to provide a general picture of the intraplant situation. Three groups of workers may be broadly identified in the terms on which their selection is based. First of all there are the koin (literally, "persons who work"), the factory's wage workers, who have had a minimum of education. There is another broad group, shokuin ("persons in charge"), paid a salary and holding clerical and supervisory positions. In this shokuin group those persons who are high school graduates and occupy lower level positions are distinguished from those who are college graduates occupying higher positions and eligible for the topmost rank.

In contrast to the American practice it must be emphasized that recruitment directly from schools into the company is to all intents and purposes the only way in which men enter the firm. When young Japanese businessmen are asked what they would do if offered a better position at more pay in another firm the general reaction is blank silence, a result of the fact that such an eventuality is so improbable—

both the offer of another position and the possibility of accepting were
it offered—that there is no response. The reaction from the more imag-
inative or speculative young man is amusement and interest in the possibility, followed by a flat and emphatic explanation that this is not
going to happen and has not happened. This is, of course, another example of the immobility of personnel that heightens the importance of the
educational system in the recruitment process.

To indicate the general methods of recruitment and their implications, the procedures actually followed in a representative company
will be described. Typical of most firms, the hiring of clerical and future supervisory personnel in this particular large company is handled
not by the local plant, as the laborers, but by the main office of the
company; and, as with many other firms, the parent office is located in
Tokyo, some distance from any of the firm's factories. The personnel
department is divided so as to provide an entirely separate staff for the
two broad groups of employees, koin and shokuin. The selection of
university graduates especially is watched most closely by top management and, in a sense, by the nation, for October, the examination month
for the companies, is a critical time for many families throughout the
nation.

Since the school year extends from spring to spring, rather than from
fall to spring as in the United States, the process of selecting the young
men who will some day manage the plant and company ordinarily begins
in early fall from among those university students who will graduate in
the spring. The procedures within each company are well defined.
Most companies have a definite policy of not accepting applications
directly from the individual job hunter. This firm considers about 40
college students yearly as candidates for employment. The company

makes known to selected universities the number and type of openings available in the firm, and it is the prerogative of the university faculty to recommend individuals for examination by the company. In this firm's practice, only five of Japan's several hundred colleges and universities are considered. These five are Tokyo, Kyoto, and Hitotsubashi Universities, state supported, and Keio and Waseda Universities, two leading private institutions. (It is important to note that four of these five universities are located in Tokyo.) Selection of men for general management training and advancement to management positions is made generally from the two curricula of economics and law. Most large Japanese universities do not have a direct equivalent of the American commercial or business curriculum.

Another part of the 40 applicants accepted are drawn from the technical curricula of engineering, chemistry, and physics. In actual fact there is some difference in the selection procedure for these more technically trained college graduates. The company feels that in these curricula the professors come to know the competence and capacity of their students better than in the larger classes of the liberal arts curricula. As a result, a lesser number of candidates are selected, and the recommendation of the professor is nearly always sufficient for hiring. With these technically trained men the important factor in selection is not merely the university attended but the professor under whom the student has studied. The company looks for its electrical engineers from among the students of one professor at one university, and for its chemists among the students of a certain professor at another university. It is the prerogative and responsibility of these leading professors to allocate their students among the several large companies.

Final selection from among these 40 applicants accepted for further testing comes in October, and a quite elaborate battery of tests is employed, including a thorough physical examination. The large Japanese factory, including this one and all others observed, employs no one suffering any kind of physical disability. A family and personal history is also obtained. The core of the testing situation, however, is a series of intellectual examinations. To illustrate these a few of the questions employed are as follows:

A. Write an essay on freedom and regulation in economic life.

B. Discuss three of the following:
   1. Technological unemployment
   2. Liquid assets
   3. Variable capital and constant capital
   4. Proxy and mandate
   5. Conversion of public debt

C. Translate into Japanese the underlined sentences:
   [In English] Human beings differ profoundly in regard to the tendency to regard their lives as a whole. To some men it is natural to do so, and essential to happiness to be able to do so with some satisfaction. To others life is a series of detached incidents without directed movement and without unity. I think the former sort are more likely to achieve happiness than the latter since they will gradually build up those circumstances from which they can derive satisfaction and self-respect, whereas the others will be blown about by the wind of circumstance now this way, now that, without ever arriving at any haven. The habit of viewing life as a whole is an essential part both of wisdom and of true morality, and is one of the things which ought to be encouraged in education.

Questions A and B are of the type asked graduates of the law and economics curricula; and for them are substituted more technical questions on their specialities for would-be engineers and research men. On the whole, however, these examples will serve to illustrate the type and level of the company-given employment tests.

There can be no question of the severity of the screening based on these tests and, inasmuch as the testing is coupled with interviews, usually with selected members of the top management group, which also weigh heavily in the final selection, there can be little doubt that the 10 or 12 men finally hired from among these 40 candidates are indeed able. The question of whether they are, on the basis of the results of their tests, appropriate candidates for top management positions was not raised by management in the course of discussions of selection procedures. The connection between competence on this kind of test and managerial skill is certainly not a necessary one.

The example cited from this firm brings out the over-all approach to the selection of college graduates. These men are taken from a sharply limited number of universities. Their very chance to apply for a job is dependent on their relations with their university professors. While in some companies more use is made of interviews, where the candidates are intensively examined by a group of ten or more members of top management, whether the interviews or tests are the prime instrument of selection, emphasis is placed on knowledge of a quite specialized sort. The examinations are designed to eliminate rather than measure, to reduce the numbers of candidates rather than probe out adequate candidates from a large group.

Looking now at the selection of high school graduates, the same company will be used to continue the illustration of Japanese recruitment and selection procedures. High school candidates in this firm are drawn from a wider geographical range of schools than are the college graduates. About 100 high schools are considered by the company to be of a level adequate to provide company employees. The company assumes that able students in the metropolitan areas will go on to college and that the candidates for employment from urban areas who have no college ambitions are seldom worth the company's attention. Thus these future clerical workers, male and female, are recruited largely from nonurban high schools. Less than one-third come from the Kobe-Osaka area in which this company has most of its facilities; the rest come from a wide scattering of prefectures. Like the college graduates, these high school students are hired through the company's main offices and are assigned to the separate factories by the main office personnel department. There is an interesting difference in the general procedure, however. In connection with the hiring of college graduates the company makes known to certain universities its needs and wants in personnel; with high school graduates the principal of the school and the teachers approach the company asking that their student or students be considered as applicants for clerical positions. These men usually take some part of their summer vacation for this activity, and the placement of good students in good positions is seen as one of their responsibilities.

This firm examines 150 high school graduates annually, and from this number about fifteen new employees are selected. The selection procedures are similar to those used for college students, again employing a battery of rather difficult academic examinations along with a physical examination and a more routine interview. Since the present high school system is comparatively new it is not possible to demonstrate statistically what appears to be a fact, that at present high school

graduates are not considered eligible for higher managerial positions.
This statement does not say that no exceptions to the college graduate
rule may be found, but that they are very few in number, usually products of the older higher schools and well known throughout the company. It might be predicted that unless the older system of education
is reinstituted, which is a real possibility, there will arise in time, and
there is now in the process of development, a formally tripartite division of workers replacing the present dichotomy of koin and shokuin.
Indeed, such a process seems well formulated in the National Railway
Company; a few graduates of the top universities are hired annually
for special positions with special income and training and assurance
that they will some day become at least divisional superintendents.

Looking at the other group in the factory, the koin, and their entrance to the company, it is hard at present to generalize on admissions
policies. At the present time few large Japanese factories are accepting new employees at this level. The problems of the work force size
discussed above are such that general employment in the factory is virtually at a standstill, except for two groups. One is the apprentice
group, still numerous in most plants, and the other is the temporary
worker described above. Most managements consider themselves for-
tunate if they can restrict admissions at the worker level to a number
no greater than the rate of retirement. Inasmuch as the "rationalization" effort sharply lowered the age level in many plants, retirements
are few. Since workers do not quit unless they are leaving factory work
entirely, there is at present little occasion to hire any large number of
permanent employees.

It may, however, be assumed that the general attitude and methods
governing the employment of apprentices are similar to those used in

the employment of general factory laborers. A plant of the firm described here has as apprentices about 60 men and 100 women. The
larger number of women is necessary to balance the higher turnover
rate in female employees. The recruitment procedures for these future
laborers are sharply different from those for future shokuin.

The intermediary in recruitment of laborers is the work stabilization
office of the Japanese government which maintains employment offices
throughout the country, and it is through these that members of the factory's personnel department contact potential employees. Only graduates of middle school are considered as candidates. Graduates of higher
school are not wanted, although the personnel department believes that
some 20 or 30 of the plant's 3,000 laborers have successfully disguised
their higher school backgrounds and are now working as laborers. The
policy of hiring minimally educated laborers is closely connected with
the other major consideration of the company in employing new laborers—what has been phrased by the personnel department as a desire
for persons with "stable natures." To find such persons, a considerable
search is made for young men just out of middle school (aged 14 or 15)
who are the sons of farmers, living in rural areas, and strongly desirous
of finding urban, factory employment.

Some trouble is gone to at the present time to find these "stable"
young men and women. For example, about 10 per cent of the current
class of apprentices were recruited from Japan's southernmost major
island, Kyushu, and from a particular agricultural area there. The
company's experience with people from this area has been good; and,
as a result, it sends representatives to the local employment office to
recruit apprentices for employment in the distant cities. Candidates
for laboring positions receive interviews and tests appropriate to their

educational level but not less severe in length and intensity than those for higher positions. Included in this test battery is a brief paper-and-pencil intelligence and dexterity test.

Unlike the shokuin, the apprentice laborers are hired by the individual factories on the decision of the local personnel department. While the shokuin are transferred from factory to factory as needed and are assigned out of the main offices, the koin will remain in the plant for which they are hired for the remainder of their careers. Although it is possible for these apprentice laborers to be fired during the first several months of their employment as apprentices, they receive full status as permanent employees. They are under the supervision of long-service foremen, live together in the company dormitories, and in general are closely supervised and thoroughly integrated into the company from about the age of 15. As stated earlier, under present factory conditions not only this factory but also most other large plants are now hiring laborers only through this apprentice route, except for the temporary employees hired and fired as the work load demands.

It might be appropriate at this point to mention the recruitment of temporary employees, who are, of course, all laborers. As the apprentices, they are hired through the work stabilization offices of the government, and here, too, the company strongly prefers temporary employees from rural backgrounds. Experience is not necessary and these temporary workers are usually farm laborers, surplus agricultural labor, who ostensibly at least are to return to the farms when the company dismisses them, their term of employment averaging about five months. They are selected by members of the personnel department who first notify the government office in desired rural districts and then interview applicants in the local offices. In addition to the inevitable phy-

sical examination, the interview deals primarily with the man's personal background. He should have an average background, with a living standard "not too high and not too low"; he should not appear rest-
less and should have a stable job history; and his education should not
be too limited but must not exceed the present middle school level.

The preceding paragraphs have described the recruitment and selection methods in one Japanese factory, a firm quite representative of the
general approach in the large Japanese manufacturing firms. The factors considered have been almost entirely formal ones, explicit and
formalized requirements for admission into employment and thus into
the permanent factory-worker relationship that distinguishes Japanese
industry, but informal factors do play a part. Such matters, however, as
family background, personality, and influential connections have their
primary influence in terms of educational level achieved and play, insofar as could be determined, a distinctly secondary role in the actual
employment process.

Still, nepotism and the like are factors in the employment system of
the Japanese factory. In many cases the large Japanese company dis-
courages and attempts to limit direct family relations among employees.
For example, marriage among employees, most particularly among
shokuin, is disapproved, and usually husband and wife may not both
continue working for the company. Not only is the wife expected to
retire, but also the husband may find that the marriage has a markedly
negative effect on his career progress. Although such marriages seem
to have increased slightly since the war, they are still few in number.

In a survey of one plant, about one out of four of the male workers
in both factory and office and about one out of four of the female
workers reported relatives in the employ of the company. This figure

is probably somewhat higher than the average. The relationship was not often father-son or father-daughter but in the majority of cases was one of uncle-nephew or uncle-niece. Especially among female office workers—better educated and from higher status families—the presence of a family member in the work situation is seen by the family at least as most desirable. The bonds of obligation between brothers in the Japanese family help account for the high incidence of uncle-niece relations in the plant.

In addition to general disapproval of close relatives in the same work situation, two factors help depress the number of such cases. First, all new employees are subject to the same tests and interviews, and these eliminate a certain number of familial candidates. Second, it is held and operates as a negative factor that the son of a worker is unable or unwilling to advance himself educationally, and he is not considered a good employment risk.

The influence of family connections seems about the same for top management positions at the present time as for workers. In large firms direct family connections are not and have not been the rule, at least since the postwar changes in ownership and management of the large companies. In the two large firms in which this problem was investigated in some detail (and with some difficulty) about two out of ten of the top management group were directly related, as sons or nephews, to former or present top managers. These cases were those in which the father or uncle had previously been himself at the very top of the management hierarchy in the firm.

This proportion is most deceptive, however. Entrance to the very few universities from which it is possible to move into top management positions is largely confined to those students whose educational and

financial resources are well above average. That is, a considerable
selection of "young men from good backgrounds" takes place without
the industrial firms themselves becoming directly involved in the process. By confining management recruitment to a limited number of
universities, the importance of family background has already been
magnified. Family connections operate in still another way, and to
illustrate this the firm discussed previously might again be used. It will
be recalled that about 40 college graduates are considered for employment annually. While the majority of these are contacted on the recommendation of professors from the key universities, a certain number,
estimated by the personnel department at 2 or 3 per year and probably
more, are considered as candidates on the urging of important custo-
mers of the firm or officials of this or related firms. These young men
must be graduates of the designated universities and must undergo the
usual testing procedure, but the personnel officials admit that the
company is placed in an awkward position if these specially recom-
mended candidates fail their examinations.

In other words, the working of family influence is commonly indirect in the large Japanese firm, but is very considerable looking at
the total recruitment process. Formally, most of the large zaibatsu
groupings have not yet re-amalgamated, although the process of re-
grouping is well under way. Even without formal or official connections, however, relations between these formerly interowned firms are
intimate and friendly. As a result, while the top official of a manufacturing firm might find it awkward to provide a position for his son in
his own company, he is able to accommodate the sons of friends or
relatives and to arrange for a position of some importance for his own
son or nephew in a related firm. Thus the son of the former president

of a chemical company might now be an official in a trading company, one which previously was directly connected with the chemical company but which is now formally independent and separate.

The full working out of all informal factors, including that of nepotism, in the recruitment and selection process, which would require the most detailed case studies of a large number of individuals, was beyond the compass of this study. Within these limits, however, the recruitment procedures when taken together with that special relationship between worker and firm described in the preceding chapter have important effects both on the internal functioning of the Japanese factory and for the nation as a whole. Seen most broadly, this system of recruitment does not fit well the present educational system in Japan and presents serious problems for the nation as a result of this lack of fit.

To review generally the differences in prewar and postwar educational scheduling, primary schools were attended by all under both systems. At primary school graduation a division took place in the older system, and the majority of youths, those with no chance to go on to higher school or college, attended a special middle school or a terminal higher primary school. These schools had the clear objective of providing the basic education for persons who would become farmers, laborers, and the like. Alternatively, youths whose families intended sending them to higher school or college went directly from primary to a general middle school.

Following middle school a division again took place in the older system between future college and noncollege students. About half of the middle school graduates attended a special higher school, usually to learn a trade; the half of the middle school students who planned university work attended a higher school designed to prepare them for college entrance.

It will be seen that the fit of the older system of education to the factory system of recruitment was a good one. Business firms received from the old-system higher primary schools individuals with a terminal lower level of education. At the present time, owing in part at least to the mixed objectives of middle school education, terminal for one group and preparatory for another, many businessmen feel their workers are not well prepared for factory work. In a nation where the average income is about forty dollars monthly, education for children beyond the middle school level is a luxury few farming or laboring families feel they can afford. Thus the pattern of high school graduation common in America is not achieved in Japan except in a limited number of cases, and the utility of the American high school in holding potential workers off the job market for a long period of time cannot be achieved in Japan.

More critical than the other tensions arising from the lack of fit of the educational system to the work system is that which occurs at the college level. In Japan for many years university graduation conferred on the student the privilege of employment at a high level in business, the military, or the government. The student expected such employment, and at the same time the pool of unemployed intellectuals that has plagued other non-Western nations did not develop. This system required, of course, a limited number of highly selected and trained university students. The increase in colleges resulting from the upgrading of former higher schools to college status has increased many times over the number of university and college students. They are not employable at the higher white-collar level owing to sheer numbers, and yet the attitude and expectations of both students and employers remain as before: college graduates are suitable for a certain kind of position only. Business firms formally, and government agencies informally, generally limit their recruitment for potential management positions at the present time to a small number of top-rated universities. The result is both a great increase in the number of unemployed college graduates and a furious competition for entrance to the few highly ranked universities. However the notion may seem to Americans, in the present Japanese context it is not bizarre for a student to commit suicide after repeatedly failing to achieve admission to a top university, despite the two or even three years spent after graduating from higher school in preparation for the entrance examinations.

This broad sketch will serve perhaps to indicate the nature of some of the issues raised for the nation by the critical role of education in Japanese industrial recruitment. Returning now to the factory itself, two main effects may be noted at this point. The first is the effect of the recruitment system on the use of personnel in the factory and, second, the effects of the recruitment system on relationships within the plant.

It has been seen that once employed a worker expects to remain indefinitely in the employ of the firm. He has been selected with some care, and once selected he is a permanent member of the firm until the end of his working career. In this system, once the worker has been selected, the company practically speaking foregoes the right to find the worker incompetent. He was not selected for a particular job or because he had acquired a particular set of skills useful in the operation of the plant. He was selected for qualities of background, personality, and general ability that may not in fact make him a competent employee. However, should the firm find him useless it cannot dismiss him but may only move him from job to job within the general category of his employment status until he is placed in a harmless and perhaps not useful position. Thus a young middle school graduate, once accepted into the worker-firm relationship, may finally become a sweeper or doorkeeper for reason of limited ability. A college graduate may be placed in a position as assistant to the least important section head and kept there for lack of ability. In any event, once admitted into employment, employees of Japanese firms will not be fired on grounds of lack of ability.

The consequences of this system in terms of efficient use of personnel need hardly be described. The proliferation of positions, the development of make-work jobs, and the loss of productivity from the retention of incompetent personnel are all clear and predictable. Conversely, the employee finding the company incompatable with his interests or ambitions or his work distasteful may not leave—except, of course, to enter a family business, return to the family farm, or open a small shop.

Another far-reaching effect of this system of recruitment within the company is its tendency to make for widely disparate groups of employees who are homogeneous within each group in experience and outlook but ill equipped to communicate with each other. This system also has effects in terms of loss of potential leadership in the lower ranks by exclusion of koin from promotion to higher status, a point which will be examined further in terms of the internal career system of the factory. It may be noted now that the recruitment system establishes three groups of employees. Each group is made up of individuals from similar backgrounds and training. The groups are markedly dissimilar each from the other.

There is, first of all, a group of workers recruited from the middle schools of Japan. These workers are usually from rural backgrounds and from lower-status families. They are employed in a particular factory, are trained together for work in that factory, and enter a similar status in the factory as apprentices and unskilled laborers.

At the other extreme in the factory status system is that group of employees who are all graduates of universities and of the same or closely related universities. Whatever their place of origin, all of these employees have spent some years in a large urban center, almost always Tokyo. They enter the firm at the same level, and their identifications and loyalties are to the firm rather than to a particular factory. Their family backgrounds are at least middle class, and they are for the most part the sons of professional people, businessmen, or higher status white-collar workers. In nearly all respects—family background, style of life, life chances, experience, and education—there are few points of contact or mutual attitudes, objectives, or experiences between this group and the first group of employees.

Somewhat intermediate to these two groups are those workers graduated from present-day higher schools, who are from a scattering of localities, often urban, sons and daughters of skilled workers and lower level white-collar workers, a more heterogeneous group sharing few of the experiences and characteristics of the extremes.

This outline of the recruitment and selection process in the Japanese factory is important to an understanding of the factory in two ways. In the first place, the system of recruitment is a part of and a reinforcement to the effects of the basic system of worker-firm relationships described earlier. Moreover, an understanding of the methods of recruitment and selection is essential to the understanding of the kinds of relationships within the firm and factory. The problems of pay and reward, career patterns and promotion opportunity, and interchange of obligations and responsibilities between employee and firm must be seen against the background of this approach to employee recruitment.

4

REWARDS AND INCENTIVES IN THE JAPANESE FACTORY

In any society or group the behaviors and modes of conduct most highly valued may be estimated by the degree to which those behaviors are rewarded by the group. The system of rewards may be examined to indicate both the kinds of behavior that the group hopes to elicit from its members and the kinds of behaviors which, through the system of reward, will be reinforced and perpetuated in the group. The study of the system of rewards and incentives employed in the large Japanese factory proved to be highly revealing of differences between Western and modern Japanese industry. It also served to demonstrate both the type and the magnitude of differences in the underlying attitudes and behaviors that differentiate modern industry in Japan from that in the United States.

In the following discussion, the pay system of one factory will be examined in detail to illustrate certain central tendencies observed in all the plants studied. Inasmuch as the system of monetary pay for work performed is only a part of the total system of rewards, the general pattern of extramonetary benefits, welfare activities, and worker incentive programs will be examined, again using specific programs and costs from particular plants. In addition, a typical retirement program will be outlined. On the basis of this data a general summary of the underlying features of the Japanese system will be undertaken and an effort will be made to compare the systems of rewards in Japan and the United States. Although there has been a good deal of discussion comparing wage levels in the two countries, most particularly with respect to textile production, these comparisons can be accurately made only when the entire wage program and reward system of the Japanese factory is examined.

The firm that will be used as an illustrative case study of the Japanese pay system is a metals-processing firm, employing some 3,400 persons, located in the Osaka-Kobe area. This firm is a relatively large one in Japan, a major producer in its field, and produces about half of its production for export. It is related to one of the large industrial combinations of prewar Japan. In short, it is an important and reputable company, and in both management policy and union history presents no special features obscuring the present over-all discussion.

As in the firm previously described there are two groups of company employees, shokuin and koin; but the koin group is further divided in this firm into monthly and daily paid workers (that is, workers whose wages are computed on the basis of daily or monthly pay). Workers with one year's seniority are promoted from the daily to the monthly paid group. Temporary workers numbered only 56 at the time of the study. The average age of all employees was 35.6 years, with 10.4 years the average length of service (wartime interruptions accounting for the relatively low average length of service).

As in all large Japanese plants, the pay system here is complicated. The reference point in the system of calculation is a fixed amount which is termed base, or standard, pay. All factory laborers begin as daily paid koin in this plant. Their initial base pay is a function of age at the time of entrance, with about 54 yen paid to workers aged 14 years and about 94 yen paid those 22 years of age or more. The initial base pay of employees hired as <u>shokuin</u> is a function of education, with a monthly base pay of 3,950 yen for graduates of the old university system, 3,700 yen monthly for graduates of the new university system, and 2,500 yen monthly for new-system high school graduates. (At the time of this study [1956], the rate of exchange was 360 yen for one U. S. dollar.) Base or standard pay accounted for about 27 per cent of the total monthly income of workers and staff in this plant, and it is in the complex increments to the base pay that a further understanding of the Japanese factory's reward system lies.

This plant, and it is typical, pays a series of additional allowances, based on factors bearing no relation to work performance or factory output, which comprise the larger portion of the worker's income. The first is the so-called work allowance, an additional 105 per cent of base pay for staff and monthly paid workers and 125 per cent for daily paid workers. The second allowance is based on attendance. Twenty-nine yen are paid to all employees for each day's attendance. Another allowance, identical for all grades of workers, is the family allowance—800 yen paid monthly for the first family member; 400 yen monthly for each of the second, third, and fourth family members; and 200 yen monthly for each additional member beyond the fourth.

A more substantial allowance than those listed so far is the age allowance, a salary increment based on age alone. The scale of payment differs slightly for staff employees and laborers, starting at 950 yen for staff employees eighteen years of age and under and increasing to 2,750 yen monthly for staff employees aged forty-one and over. For <u>koin</u> the scale begins at a slightly lower figure—750 yen at age eighteen and under and increasing to the same amount as the staff, 2,750 yen, for persons aged forty-one years or more. This age allowance accounts for about 10 per cent of the total salaries paid in this factory.

The work, attendance, family, and age allowances by no means exhaust the list of increments to base pay. Staff employees receive a somewhat ambiguously titled "temporary," or "special," allowance. It is paid at the rate of 90 per cent of the base pay of each staff employee. This scale has apparently been developed to balance the payment to laborers of a productivity allowance, which is determined in this plant by a seemingly complex formula: the worker's monthly base rate of pay is divided by 30 and this figure is multiplied by the "efficiency" of the plant for the pay period. Most of the larger factories, although conspicuously lacking in the time-study methods and detailed cost analyses known in the United States, have derived a base figure for "efficiency," usually referred to as standard output. When output exceeds this standard figure the plant is said to be operating at more than base efficiency; and from this estimate is derived the basis for paying the laborers a productivity allowance. Examination of pay records indicated that the output in large companies generally exceeds the standard output rate. Consequently, the large plants nearly always pay a productivity allowance. The allowance remains remarkably stable in amount and may be taken—in fact, clearly is taken—to be a regular part of the worker's income.

A further allowance is paid in this plant—a job-rank allowance. It will be noted that there is no provision in the above-mentioned pay schedules for differences in actual work done. Such payment differentiated by job is also calculated on the base or standard pay. The increment for the shokuin is from 10 to 30 per cent for persons in "responsible positions," that is, for people occupying the positions of chief of section, department, or plant; for the koin, the increment for persons in positions of responsibility is 10 per cent, and 20 per cent for workers in very dangerous or highly skilled jobs.

Companies with several factories in various parts of the country pay an additional allowance. It is a "regional" allowance to adjust for differences in living costs in the different locations. A note should be added to this review of the complicated wage system employed in this metals-processing factory. The given figures for base pay are those for persons at the time of entering the plant—derived from age for laborers and education for staff employees. These base or standard wages are increased regularly, once a year for staff people and twice annually for laborers. The increase for staff employees can range from 60 to 390 yen monthly if the total base wage is less than 7,000 yen; an increase of 150 to 260 yen is considered standard. The range for individuals whose base pay is over 7,000 yen monthly is from 60 to 450 yen. The semi-annual increase for the koin is 93 yen monthly and for daily paid laborers 2 yen, 50 sen per day.

An over-all view of the net effect of this system of payment is given in Table 2. It shows the amount paid shokuin and koin in total, by allowances, and the per cent each allowance contributes to the total wage paid. As Table 2 indicates, pay for overtime work is no small fraction of the total salary. Although it is not usually paid at premium rates in this plant, a 25 per cent premium is paid for overtime work on production that is "needed urgently" and for work between the hours of 10:00 P.M. and 5:00 A.M. A 25 per cent premium is also paid for holiday work. When shifts are used, the 2nd and 3rd shifts of workers are paid, respectively, a 15 and 30 per cent increment to their normal daily pay.

Table 2

MONTHLY WAGES AND TYPE OF PAYMENT

Type of Payment	Shokuin		Koin	
	Amount (Yen)	Per Cent	Amount (Yen)	Per Cent
Base Pay	6,390	27.5	4,751	26.7
Work allowance	7,673	33.1	4,604	25.8
Temporary allowance	5,741	24.8		
Productivity allowance			5,028	28.2
Age allowance	1,835	7.9	1,982	11.1
Family allowance	956	4.1	1,367	7.7
Attendance allowance	678	2.9	693	3.9
Miscellaneous			367	2.1
Deductions	– 69	– 0.3	– 980	– 5.5
Subtotal	23,204	100.0	17,812	100.0
Overtime	3,498	15.1	4,847	27.2
TOTAL	26,702		22,659	

In sum, the average staff employee in the plant is paid the equivalent of about seventy-five dollars monthly; the average laborer's wage is about sixty-five dollars monthly.[1] Since women in this and other plants receive substantially lower average salaries by virtue of their younger age, lesser education, and lower positions, these figures are somewhat deceptive. A comparison of the salaries of men and women

[1] The universally paid semi-annual bonus is not included in these figures. (See pp. 72-73.)

in this plant shows that staff men receive about 32,000 yen monthly and staff women about 13,000; male laborers receive about 23,000 yen monthly and female laborers about 13,000.

Although Japanese government statistics are not always reliable, it would appear from a comparison with recent government estimates that pay in this plant is well above the national average for manufacturing industries, which is slightly over 50 dollars monthly for male employees and slightly over 20 dollars monthly for female employees. We are discussing here, however, large factories of well-established firms, and only those where firsthand data was collected. Among the firms observed, the pay scale in this plant was in the upper half but was not the highest.

Wages are paid for a 7-hour working day which begins at 8:00 A.M. and continues until 4:00 P.M., with one hour for lunch. Overtime, which is desired and expected by the workers, is limited to a maximum of 50 hours each month. Sunday is the one nonwork day of the week, but many holidays are given during the year. For instance, there are 5 national holidays; a week's vacation during the New Year's period is granted all workers; May Day and a religious festival day at the company shrine are also holidays for the entire plant; shokuin receive an additional 20 and koin 15 days annually; and paid holidays are given for marriage (5 days), childbirth (42 days), deaths of family members (2 to 7 days, depending on the relationship to the deceased), anniversaries of the death of spouse, children, or parents, and severe illness of close relatives (up to 10 days). Time off is also allowed for the performance of public duties and in the event of a calamity of natural cause. Although this imposing list of paid nonworking days is not complete, it gives a notion of the wide range of reasons for holidays. The working regulations are not, on the whole, onerous.

In summary, the worker in this factory, excluding holidays, works about 9 hours a day (including overtime), six days a week, and receives about sixty-five dollars a month for his efforts. The preceding paragraphs, however, do not describe the entire picture of reward and recompense in the large Japanese factory; and there remains an important series of extra-pay factors to be considered. Since it reveals much of the underlying rationale of worker-firm relations in Japan, it needs to be examined closely.

First of all, the pay system rests on the base-pay formula, which is not set by the kind of work done, the efficiency with which the work is performed, or the worker's capacity to perform his or other work. Base pay is a function of age and education, and only of these factors. Although some moderate latitude is allowed for competence and advantage, further increments to the base pay are primarily a function of length of service. In actual practice it appears that little use is made of the latitude in base pay increments, with pay raises almost uniform for each age group. About 10 per cent of the total pay is a direct function of age and, since the work allowance is a per cent increment to base pay, this work allowance too is largely a product of age and education. Indeed, the entire salary is largely based on the employee's educational status on entering the company and the length of time he has served. The exceptions are the family allowance, quite irrelevant to factory performance, the attendance allowance, hardly a critical test of job competence, and the job-rank allowance which alone is related closely to the nature of the work performed. In other words, only a small part of the total reward of the Japanese worker depends on the kind of work he does and the way in which he does it. This

fact has far-reaching implications in terms of both systems of production and systems of human relations. Its importance is underlined when
the examination of the reward system proceeds from the direct monetary
rewards to the total range of rewards and incentives provided the Japanese worker.

Data obtained in another specific plant will be used to illustrate
the further range of the system of reward and its importance in the total
worker compensation scheme in Japan. This plant is a textile manufacturing plant which employs 3,500 workers, about one-third of whom
are women. The average age of the male worker is 30 years, that of
the women 23 years, and the average length of service is about 7 years.
Table 3 presents the budget for a one-month period of the welfare activities carried out for the laborers in this plant.

An appreciation of the magnitude of the expenditure may be gained
by comparing the net sum of 11,000,000 yen expended for welfare activities with the total payroll of 50,405,000 yen for the same month.
The welfare program in this plant represents a 20 per cent increment to
the total direct labor payment.

Some of the items listed in Table 3 warrant a closer look. First of
all, the company provides meals in the company cafeteria for all employees during working hours, usually the noon meal, for which the
worker pays 30 yen (about 8 cents). If he lives in a dormitory he can
eat his other meals at a similar cost. Thus a young worker in this company can eat at his accepted standard for about 7 dollars per month.
His room, shared with others in the dormitory, which has a game room,
dining room, laundry, and other facilities, will cost him 155 yen (less
than 50 cents) each month. The staff for the dining rooms and dormitories are company personnel. The public bath, a popular institution in

Table 3

MONTHLY BUDGET OF A WELFARE PROGRAM IN A TEXTILE PLANT

(Thousands of Yen)

Type of Activity	Total Cost	Total Income
Meals	3,422	1,758
Dormitories	4,720	15
Bath	48	0
Company houses	1,225	187
Kindergarten	83	14
Company store	481	618
Schools	282	0
Library	54	0
Dormitory clubs	260	2
Park	66	7
Hospital and health	3,954	812
TOTAL	14,595	3,413

Japan, is provided and maintained in the factory area by the company at no cost to the workers. Haircuts and shampoos may be obtained in the company barbershop. The company store sells articles such as toilet goods and clothing at about 10 per cent below market cost. Since the company maintains a well-equipped and well-staffed dental and medical center, the worker's medical expenses are almost nil. Athletic facilities exist in considerable number, and the dormitory has an extensive and active club system to provide entertainment. The worker is most likely to spend his holidays at the mountain or beach dormitory maintained by the company, for which he will be charged a small fee.

In short, nearly every detail of his life is interpenetrated by the company's facilities, guidance, and assistance.

When a young man in this textile plant marries he receives other benefits. If he is from a distant village he will probably live in a company house where his monthly rent will be slightly higher than in the dormitory—probably about 700 yen. His wife receives medical attention from the company clinic at one-quarter of full cost and purchases most nonfood items for the home from the company store. If the worker lives some distance from the plant his costs of commuting will be shared by the company. At the time of his marriage he receives a sum equal to about one-third of a month's wages from both the company and the cooperative to which he belongs as an employee. He will also receive financial aid in the event of illness, death, or other misfortune. His income increases with marriage, of course, and will increase still more as children are born. His children may attend the company school.

It would be tedious to provide a catalogue of the ways in which benefits and services are provided the Japanese worker quite apart from his directly paid wages. The intention here is to illustrate the kinds and the range of such indirect benefits and to indicate the involvement of the reward system of a company in the life of the worker.

In some respects the welfare program in this particular plant is more extensive than the average. For example, in an effort to increase the involvement of the individual in the company, management instituted a program of inviting parents of workers from distant villages to spend a weekend at the plant, stay in the dormitory, see their children, and learn about the company and their children's work. However, every plant observed had an elaborate program of benefits, varying somewhat with geographical and historical circumstances. Even in the large cities most plants provide company housing for at least a third of their employees. The benefits described are, of course, in addition to those required by law, such as disability insurance.

Before examining the social implications of the Japanese compensation system, two more aspects of the welfare program must be noted. The first is the retirement system used in the large factory; the second, returning to wages, is the system of bonuses by which the wage level is increased about 10 per cent.

When visiting Japanese companies, conversation repeatedly turned to a discussion of retirement age and retirement pay, asking for information about and comparing the retirement programs of American and Japanese firms. The problem is a serious one for Japanese companies, one made no less difficult by the enormous inflation of currency in the postwar period. As is clear from the description of management attitudes, Japanese management has a considerable responsibility, extending beyond the workshop, for the workers. In this kind of worker-firm relationship it is not possible to simply dismiss workers with no further concern at the end of their period of usefulness. At the same time neither the Japanese business firm nor the Japanese government has devised any system of retirement pay or allowances that would enable the worker to look ahead to a secure living after leaving the factory.

The present average retirement age in most large Japanese factories is 55 years for male employees. The age, however, sometimes differs by employee rank, higher ranked employees being allowed to work to an older age. The stated retirement age for women is usually 50 years, although in fact it would be a rare case in which a woman remained in the company's employ much beyond 30 years of age. The retirement age limit is strictly enforced except, as noted, with members of top

management. Senior executives often continue in their positions well
beyond the 55-year limit.

Looking first at the retirement system for laborers, the practice in a
specific company will be cited to indicate the kind of retirement allowance paid. Retirement pay in this company, as so many elements of the
employee's career, is based first on education and second on length of
service with the company. The company has established a base amount
for retirement depending on these two factors. Thus, for example, a
middle school graduate who retires at the company's request after 20
years of service (a most unlikely event) would receive a total of
600,000 yen. In the event of death or injury forcing retirement, the
slightly larger sum of 690,000 yen would be paid. Should the worker
of his own will decide to leave the company after 20 years of service,
he would receive the full retirement allowance; but had he left voluntarily before completing 20 years service he would receive only a
fraction of the total allowance. Table 4 shows how this system works
for the different categories of education at three levels of length of
service.

The general pattern of the retirement allowance system used in this
plant is to reward length of service in increasing proportion with time
spent with the company and to penalize voluntary retirement from the
company at an early date. Retirement allowances are not large. If a
worker who is a middle school graduate leaves the company after 30
years in its employ, he will be paid 1,713,600 yen, the equivalent
of about five years' salary. It is not a small sum, but is hardly sufficient to maintain the worker and his family from the time of retirement
to death. It is, however, a lump sum payment. As such it represents a
very considerable capital amount and is often invested in a house,

Table 4

RETIREMENT ALLOWANCES IN A JAPANESE FACTORY

Education of Worker	Length of Service (Years)	Amount of Retirement Allowance (Thousands of Yen)		
		Company's Request	Injury or Death	Worker's Request
University	5	64	64	32
	10	174	183	122
	20	960	1,104	960
Higher school	5	52	52	26
	10	140	147	98
	20	720	828	720
Middle school	5	43	43	22
	10	120	126	84
	20	600	690	600
Higher primary school	5	34	34	17
	10	92	97	64
	20	414	476	414

some part of which is then sublet, or in a small shop. The worker, however, must anticipate looking for temporary and part-time employment
following his retirement and dependency on his children for support in
old age. Given the present Japanese family system, such support may
reasonably be expected from children or relatives.

The foregoing discussion has been in terms of workers. Formally,
management retirement is similar, and it will be noted that the scale
of retirement pay offers no provision beyond the influence of education in the retirement allowance for job rank. Informally, however,
a further provision is available for more favored workers and for members of management. This is the system of affiliated or subordinate
companies whereby a large plant has a group of satellite plants closely

associated with it. The subsidiary firms often use machinery and methods drawn from the parent firm and are dependent on the parent firm for capital and for business. The management of these smaller plants as well as the supervisory staff is frequently made up largely of persons retired from the parent factory, but there is no formal rule governing such an assignment. It is one of the points at which favor and personal relations have the largest play in the system of reward.

Thus far three primary types of reward and incentive have been considered—the wage system itself, nonmonetary benefits, and the retirement allowance system. There remains still another tangible and important element in the reward system of the Japanese factory, a financial gain provided employees but one which is strictly speaking not a part of the wage system. This is the payment, usually twice anually, of a considerable bonus to all company employees. The amount of the bonus is often equivalent to one month's wages, or, during a year's period, an increment to total wages of about 15 per cent. It is ordinarily paid at mid-summer and again at the end of the year, both periods, it might be added, being traditional for the exchange of gifts in Japanese society.

The bonus is at present very much a part of the regular wage system. Employees expect a bonus and organize their living standard around the payment of a bonus. Thus expenditures for special purchases, such as a radio or washing machine, are delayed until bonus time. Since its size is a determining factor in department store sales and vacation expenditures, the nation as a whole watches with considerable attention the bonus scale for industry for the semi-annual periods.

The bonus payment for each period is the subject of extensive negotiations with the union, ordinarily over the total amount of money to be allotted for bonuses, with management enjoying the prerogative of assigning specific sums to each individual. As a result one might expect that the bonus would become a way of rewarding the individual effort of a particularly energetic or productive worker. So far as could be ascertained there is, in fact, little difference in the amount received within given groups or by specific types of employees. The differences that exist are to some extent a function of job rank, and there is virtually no differential in the amount of payment within a job grade.

One function of the bonus payment in the Japanese factory today appears to be its utility as a device for protecting from union negotiation the base wage structure of the plant. The complexities of the wage payment system are further extended by the bonus payment. Thus it is possible for management at a given time to yield to a union demand for increased compensation without altering the basic system of compensation. For example, the basic differential in wages between shokuin and koin may be left unchanged while some one of the several allowances paid, which are of course based on this differential, may be altered slightly. Or, again, the demand for higher wages can be met temporarily by increasing the amount of money assigned to bonus payment.

The system appears to be a makeshift even though it has become an integral part of the wage system in all large Japanese factories. It is an unwieldy device in all respects and has the disadvantage of requiring repeated and heated union negotiations at six-month intervals. The significance of the bonus system in this discussion is its essentially paternalistic nature. It remains, however taken for granted it may be, basically a gift from the firm to the employees of the firm, not an obligation or duty as wages must be seen. It should be emphasized that the amount of the bonus is only indirectly related to factory output or profit during a given term.

Discussion of the bonus and its paternalistic and nonrational nature in terms of the productivity goals of the factory organization brings up the related issue of management compensation in Japan. Since this study of social factors in management in Japan did not and could not extend to financial details, specific examples of detailed management compensation cannot be provided. To obtain such detailed information would have required an investigator with the training of an accountant and the instincts of a tax collector.

In general, it is true to say that the actual cash wages paid management in Japan are quite low and that the difference between managers' and workers' wages as paid in cash is not large. For example, in one large plant the factory manager received a salary of about two hundred dollars per month. However, it would be absurd to treat this sum as his actual compensation. His home, a most attractive residence by any standards, was provided by the firm and cost him some four dollars a month in rent. The firm also provided his car and chauffeur (a company employee), and may provide vacations for himself and his family in addition to a most elaborate and frequent entertainment schedule. Rumor and hearsay would assign a very considerable number of similar additional compensations to men at his level; and it is probable that the actual wages or salary paid are the smallest portion of the total compensation of top management.

The system of indirect and paternalistic compensation is not, however, confined to the very top echelons of management. For instance, a young employee of a large steel firm who held no executive rank, although clearly a candidate for future higher position, received an income of less than seventy-five dollars per month. But his five-room apartment, including utilities, made available by the company for 750 yen (about two dollars per month), and the supplementary benefits he enjoyed made comparison of this young man's income with that of a person in a comparable position in an American firm quite impossible.

As world trade becomes more competitive, comparisons of wage scales between countries, such as the United States and Japan, become more common and more heated, but they should be undertaken with some caution. It does not, in fact, seem possible to directly compare wages in the two countries in detail. The wage system described here indicates that, on a purely arithmetic basis, the actual cash wage paid is only part of the total compensation offered the worker in a large Japanese factory. If a direct comparison on a dollar-and-cents basis were to be made, some provision would be necessary for the additional allowances, benefits, and indirect payments offered the Japanese worker. Another consideration is the fact that the Japanese firm, whatever its size, guarantees to the full limit of its financial capacity continued and total employment to all of its workers. This guarantee is a major part of the total compensation in Japan, but it is a difficult one to include in an arithmetic comparison of the two wage scales. It might also be noted at this point that, although the small Japanese firm, for example, a spinning company employing perhaps 20 workers at 40 looms, pays very low cash wages to its workers, its area of responsibility for these workers is very broad. It extends even to an obligation on the part of the manager of the plant to successfully arrange marriages for the female employees before they reach the age of thirty years. Here again is a real obligation on management's part, a real compensation for employment provided the workers, and a compensation not readily assigned a monetary value.

An accurate comparison of Japanese and American wage levels is further confounded by the fact that the worker in the large Japanese factory is substantially well off in relation to the over-all Japanese standard of living. When recruiting high school students, for example, it was noted that personnel departments tended to avoid city higher schools. Since the sons and daughters of a Japanese factory worker are sufficiently well off in comparison with those of farm or other city workers they can and will attend college if they are able and intelligent. Japanese factory workers also appear very well paid when their wages are compared to those of workers in other Asian countries. It is difficult to see how comparisons of management compensation in Japan and the United States could be made. Without being able to offer detailed evidence it does seem, however, that the gap in real wages between workers and managers is as great in Japan as in the United States. When all factors are considered Japanese executives are very well repaid for their work.

An examination of the basis for the system of rewards and incentives in the Japanese factory reveals an important difference in the kinds of behaviors rewarded in comparison with the industrial system of the West. First of all, the forms of compensation are more varied and often less direct than those in American plants. Although American firms too offer benefits in forms other than immediate wages paid, these seldom go beyond such matters as insurance, annuities, and retirement allowances, which are only one step removed from an actual cash payment. Moreover, in the United States the wages paid in cash are by far the greater part of the benefits received, and it is the actual monetary wage that is used by the employee to estimate his worth to the company and his success at his job.

In the Japanese system, membership in the firm itself is no small part of the worker's recompense. Each firm has a distinctive insignia, made up in the form of a lapel button, which is a proudly worn badge of membership in a distinctive and important group. The difficulties of admission to employment and the nature of the commitment undertaken by both worker and firm at the time of employment find their counter- part in the less direct, less impersonal forms of reward. The company is held to be and considers itself responsible for the total person, includ- ing his food, clothing, and shelter, and takes a direct responsibility for providing these things, along with such items as medical care and educa- tion. Stated positively, the Western system emphasizes the impersonal exchange of job services for cash reward. Responsibility for living and health standards is an individual problem for each worker. The Japanese employee is part of a very much more personal system, a system in which his total functioning as a person is seen as management's responsibility and in which his group membership transcends his individual privileges and responsibilities.

It would not be accurate for either system to describe the Western one as coldly commercial and impersonal, the Japanese as warmly inti- mate or mutually cooperative. There is a difference between the two systems, however, and the difference extends in the direction of these two poles. It would be no less accurate to describe the Japanese system as paternalistic or, as became popular in Japan after the end of the Second World War, feudalistic. It is a feudalistic system only by anal- ogy, but it is a system in which the exchange of obligations and respon- sibilities inherent in any group interaction cannot be discharged by a solely monetary exchange.

At the risk of considerable oversimplification it might be useful to note here the logic that seems to underlie a system of payment in a

factory where that payment is related only to the view of the factory
as an organization to produce at maximum efficiency a given product.
Reward in such a system would be given in relation to the capacity of
the individual to contribute to efficient and maximal production. To
the extent that the individual failed to contribute in an amount equivalent to another individual, his reward would be proportionately lessened.
Payment would then be based on factors relating to the position an individual occupies and the extent to which he effectively fulfills the
demands of his job.

The Japanese system of reward does not operate on these kinds of
assumptions. For example, a prime factor in the payment system is the
employee's age. Although length of service might be seen as having
some relationship to job performance, justifying its importance in the
scheme of job reward, age in itself would appear to have no relationship to the job situation, except insofar as advancing age might reduce
job efficiency. This kind of nonrational reward system is more drama-
tically illustrated by the family allowance. Not only does the number
of persons in a worker's family have no connection with the goals of
the factory but also to reward, in effect, increased family membership
seems a cruel contradiction in a nation painfully subject to a high population density.

In other words, recompense in the Japanese factory is in large part
a function of matters that have no direct connection with the factory's
productivity goals. They can be termed relevant to factory pay only
when the relationship between worker and firm, and the assumptions
on which that relationship rests, are defined outside the more limited
range of productivity, output, profit, and efficiency. It is not at all
difficult to find situations where workers doing identical work at an

identical pace receive markedly different salaries, or where a skilled work-
man is paid at a rate below that of a sweeper or doorman. The position
occupied and the amount produced do not determine the reward provided.

In terms of factory efficiency two primary results obtain from this
system of payment and reward. The first is the furthering of the limitations on the mobility of the workers. The importance given to education, age, length of service, and similar factors in the total wage scale
means that the worker is heavily penalized for job mobility and strongly
rewarded for steady service. Taken together with the factors involved
in recruitment, it will be seen that labor mobility is virtually nonexist-
ent in the Japanese system. What is rewarded is the worker's loyalty
and a deep commitment to the firm.

In terms of modern production methods the reward apparatus has a
second and more immediate effect. The whole mechanism of job evaluation, cost analysis, and incentive systems can find no place in the large
Japanese factory without clashing violently with the present system.
Underlying all devices for increased productivity is the assumption that
the individual should be rewarded in relation to specified job demands
and his individual work effort. It is possible to find in the large Japanese factory some measure of wage differential by job type, usually
limited to some additional payment for extremely hazardous work, as,
for example, in shipyards and steel forges. As in the pay scales cited
above, it is also possible to find some recompense on a group basis for
productivity. These two examples are, however, minor exceptions to the
general rule that job output does not govern wage level. More important,
as has been noted, individual effort is not a component of wage calculation. It is seldom possible to identify and isolate individual competence or individual job responsibility in the Japanese factory.

In devices such as time and motion study the individual's skill and speed are under constant scrutiny. Although informal group pressures may govern the worker's particular reactions, the fact remains that his pay and his progress in the plant are partly based on and always susceptible to measurement in terms of his individual output. A thoroughgoing system of cost analysis demands this kind of precision in the calculation of output. It is perhaps not too much to say that in the American firm the underlying assumption of incentive methods is one of individual responsibility to which the informal group makes certain adaptations. In the Japanese factory, however, it is group work and group output that measure success, with only some minor accommodations to individual differences.

It is on this general point that many of the efforts to introduce new, usually American-style methods into the Japanese firm flounder. Japanese engineers and managers who attempt to introduce quality control and cost analysis into a plant sometimes find themselves unable to obtain the necessary information and support; American technicians fail to communicate successfully what it is they are trying to accomplish. In both situations the difficulty appears to stem from the fact that Western methods rely on assumptions about the nature of the work experience which are not valid for the Japanese work situation.

In attempting to summarize the general differences between the reward systems in the large Japanese factories and those in comparable American production units, it is apparent that the definitions of the work situation and the nature of the work experience differ. The qualities on which recompense is based in the Japanese factory are those broad social considerations—such as age, education, and number of family members—which can be seen as relevant to work compensation only if the nature of the work group is viewed in a way different from that in the United States. Membership in this work group rests on general considerations of character and background. It is a permanent membership. Reward is thus related to fidelity to the group and to the needs of the individual as husband and father. Motivation for work output rests in large part on loyalty and group identification. In terms of motivation and reward, the group operates in a context quite different from that of the American work unit, one more nearly akin to our family groupings.

5

RANK, CAREERS, AND THE FORMAL ORGANIZATION

To obtain a perspective on the underlying nature of the social organization of the large Japanese factory, it is useful to look briefly into the surroundings and organization of some of the myriad small production units of Japan. There are revealed in these small factories, employing only a few people, elements that are hard to discern in the giant and complex factory units. In the small factory one finds the analogue and paradigm of the organization of the large factory.

Traveling from Tokyo by one of the web of electric trains that crisscross the Kanto plain, after about one hour's ride the traveler arrives in a silk spinning and weaving center, a small city of about 30,000 persons. The city is not attractive. Badly damaged by wartime bombing—there was an aircraft plant nearby—its buildings are painfully new and crowded together; the city presents a dusty, jerry-built aspect quite out of keeping with its traditional setting and traditional industry.

This city is a major producing center for silk goods, not, it is true, the elegant and expensive kimono and obi of Kyoto, but "middle-class" goods of moderate quality and price. The center of the industry is a new concrete and stucco building, quite modern in design, located on the main street of the town. This building is the headquarters of the cooperative society, which was founded in 1899 by a group of silk factory owners to provide joint services for the marketing and distribution of their products. The society is in truth cooperative. One of the many paradoxes of Japan is that a nation famous for fierce loyalties to family and clan should also have a strong and still healthy tradition, which has existed for centuries, of cooperative banks, communities, and all manner of business groups.

The 750-odd factories in this area employ a total of about 10,000 women and about 1,100 men. The smallest of the factories has three looms, operated by the owner's family; the largest, the president of which is head of the cooperative, has about 150 machines and 80 employees. The typical plant, and there are many of this type, uses about 20 machines and has 15 workers.

The factory of Mr. Watanabe will serve as an example of these many plants. Built just after the war, it is somewhat newer than the average plant, which in this city is about 15 years old. (The oldest has been in continuous operation by the same management for 50 years.) It is also slightly larger than average, with 30 looms and 19 employees. The factory, the workers' living quarters, and Mr. Watanabe's home are all enclosed in the same compound; indeed, the three units are quite inseparable and form a single work and living arrangement. The visitor enters the gate and stops at the entrance to the home, where a member of the family inquires about his business. Mr. Watanabe conducts his affairs in the family living room overlooking the yard, which is not only a playground for his children and the family's pets but also the space for hanging the drying silk after it has been dyed.

The workers in the factory are essentially an extension of the Watanabe family. The 15 women employees are young girls, aged fifteen to twenty-two years. They are from farm homes in the surround-

ing villages and their employment has been arranged between Mr.
Watanabe and their parents. They live in a wing of the family house,
their food is prepared jointly with that of the family, and special holidays and occasions are enjoyed by the entire group, both family and
workers. Mr. Watanabe's responsibilities for them extend beyond those
of an employer in a comparable small establishment in the United States.
He, in fact, acts in loco parentis. He provides care, advice, and coun-
sel for his workers and, finally—no small part of his duties as factory
owner—arranges or assists in the arrangement of their marriages. The
girls enter the plant immediately after middle school graduation, serve
a three year apprenticeship, and then, usually after two additional
years of work, marry.

The workshop itself is a crowded, noisy, loom-filled room presided
over by an older man, a foreman. There are other men on the payroll:
a mechanic charged with maintenance of the machines; a silk specialist who supervises the quality of the material, its handling, and the
designs produced; and a young boy learning the trade who acts as messenger and general handyman. Each of the girls in the shop is responsible for two looms, set facing each other, between which she stands at
her work. The atmosphere of the shop is one of steady, rather rapid
work, but at the same time there is a good deal of conversation, jok-
ing, and moving around within the group of girls.

From the background of publicity and controversy in the United
States one might well ask if this plant is a sweatshop and if these girls
are slave laborers. In a sense the answer to both questions is yes. The
niceties of labor laws governing wages, hours, unionization, and similar factors do not penetrate the shop with any regularity. Apart from
provision for insurance as required by law and occasional visits by a

government inspector, this is the exclusive fiefdom of Mr. Watanabe. The hours are governed by work demands and extend to well over 60 hours each week. The wages are low indeed, and consist largely of the food, lodging, clothing, and care provided as one would provide for a large and slightly improvident group of relatives. Nevertheless, the atmosphere is not that of a sweatshop, and the attitudes and actual relations among the people, at least in this plant, are not those of slave laborers. Relations are close and warm, and the girls have a most intimate knowledge of each other. There is little leisure, and the Sunday holiday is spent largely in small domestic tasks. The world is a most confined one, seldom extending beyond the factory compound. Undoubtedly the system can be and sometimes is perverted into a vicious and punishing sweatshop. Clearly it is not here, nor is it usually so. This interval in the workers' lives, the five or seven years between school and marriage, is part of the accepted scheme of things for these girls, an interval in which they are cared for and in which they work in a fashion not at all inconsistent with their backgrounds.

Men like Mr. Watanabe are common in this small city. He is about 50 years old and has spent all his life here, working in silk factories and training for the position he has finally attained. His success is owed to his training, to the president of the plant in which he worked, and to his present very hard work. He started ten years ago with four machines and is on his way to a most successful operation. The original four machines stood in his home and were operated by his wife and one of her relatives, while Watanabe himself was president, mechanic, messenger, and silk specialist. Since the silk industry has not prospered greatly of late, not all men who started as he did have prospered.

Looking at men in the area who do not yet have their own plants, it develops that there is both a strong desire to attempt an independent operation and a feeling that it is now, under present circumstances, nearly a hopeless goal. To begin operating a plant of the smallest size requires about 1,000,000 yen (less than 3,000 dollars), an enormous amount of capital for men in their position. Japanese banks simply do not lend venture capital to unknown and improvident men who hope to start new businesses. Their only hope is the avenue Mr. Watanabe took—to work long, faithfully, and for little money for a man who is himself the head of a silk factory. In the fullness of time and in exchange for long service, a loan will then perhaps be made. It will be a personal loan and the interest rate will exceed even the 12 per cent which is customary in Japan. The demands will be high, and the borrower who cannot meet his commitments faces total loss. About ten men annually begin operations as newly born entrepreneurs. Few survive.

Here, on a quick glance and a hurried visit, is a sketch of a large section of Japanese factory units. The community which forms the universe of a group of such units, whether city neighborhood or country town, is small and circumscribed. From long interaction and shared backgrounds and experiences, the workers in the factories are closely related. A complex web of relations knits the owner group in the community together—apprentice years, financial assistance and mutual aid, and obligations of services performed and favors rendered. The workers in turn are tied closely to the owner of the plant. He is in a very real sense their father for the period of their employment. Their world is usually limited to their own factory, and the relationship between worker and owner is made even closer by shrine visits and holidays together.

There is no intention of arguing here either that the large Japanese factory grew out of these small plants, or that the differences between factories in Japan and the West are the result of an incubation period of the large Japanese factory as this kind of unit. Large factories have their own history and a separate evolution. It is possible to say, however, that the patterns and trends which are present in more obscure form in the giant shipbuilding, steel, and chemical plants stand out in sharp relief in the small Japanese factories. At either end of the size continuum, from the plant employing only the owner's sons and daughters to that employing 10,000 persons, the social context for both kinds of units is the same. The backgrounds, attitudes, and expectations of the people in the factory contain similar elements, and the kind of organization and types of methods developed by and for dealing with these people have basic similarities. Thus Mr. Watanabe's factory provides a useful backdrop for a detailed examination of the organization and relationships of the large factory.

Management of the large firm in Japan, like its American counterpart, will often begin an explanation of its functioning with the presentation of a chart of the organization of the firm. Although the chart is useful, it must be approached with some caution by one with an American background. Whatever its seeming resemblance, there are major differences between it and an American prototype. However, for examining the formal organization of the Japanese firm and for searching out some of the factors which have shaped that organization, the chart will provide a useful guide line.

Most large Japanese firms operate in several locations. The main office is located in one of the large cities, usually in a downtown area. Since the war there has been a very strong tendency for the main office to be located in Tokyo—near the government, near the sources of capital and credit, and near the centers of foreign purchasers' offices, always an important factor in the life of the Japanese firm. The main office is the center of the primary administrative units of the firm, and the several plants, laboratories, and sales offices of the firm are scattered throughout the country.

To illustrate the central trends which appear to be common to the large firms studied, the organization of a firm manufacturing electrical equipment will be outlined. The firm employs a total of about 7,000 persons, of whom slightly less than 500 work in the main office and the remainder in its two factories and research laboratory. As in the factories of this and most other companies, the units of organization of the main office include, first, departments, divided in turn into sections which are further divided into branches. At the top of the organization is a board of directors, which in this firm includes 13 men, 6 of whom are also operating heads of units of the company. Reporting to the board of directors is the president, an auditing staff, and a legal counselor. Since the rules governing finance in large firms are substantially less demanding in Japan than in the United States, the auditors are employees of the company. The post of counselor is in many firms an honored and honorific one filled by retired senior officers of the firm. There is sometimes a considerable proliferation of the advisor and counselor positions.

The actual operating heads of the firm, the men who are usually in direct charge of the company, are entitled managing directors. In this firm there are two such positions, roughly corresponding to a vice-president of finance and a vice-president of production in the United States. The correspondence is not exact, however, since in this and

in many large firms the office of president is not an operating office.
That is, the functions of the president are largely concerned with political and social relations and with representing the firm to outside
organizations and persons. The situation is not unlike that, familiar to
students of Japanese political history, when the emperor was in fact
powerless, holding an exemplary and symbolic position with actual control vested in a military commander. In time the military commander
too became a figurehead, with control passing to a family acting as
regents for him. Without dwelling on the parallel, there is a tendency
in Japan for power to be exercised indirectly through symbolic leaders.
This tendency may be noted in the large companies, where functioning
responsibility and control seem usually to rest with the managing directors, as well as in the Japanese government. In some companies the
control function is divided into a senior managing director group and a
managing director group. In the company being considered here no
such further division has yet developed.

Reporting to the managing directors in this firm are 13 department
heads, including the heads of the 10 departments of the main office and
the heads of the two factories and the laboratory. That is, the main office department chiefs have positions equal in rank and authority to,
and separate in the organization's structure from, the operating or line
managers, which would appear, in terms of presentation on a chart, to
make for a neat separation of line and staff functions in the Japanese
factory. In actual fact, as will be seen, the staff or main office departments run parallel to the factory organization, but the line of demarca-
tion is not clear and is constantly changing. The rule-of-thumb procedure is for matters concerning the company as a whole to be decided
by the main office and those involving a local plant to be decided at

the plant level. The rule is not entirely useful. For example, both the main office and the individual plants have personnel departments. Promotions at the executive level, or above general foremen, are decided by the main office, thus extending the influence of the main office personnel department far into the local plant. Also, on a given local issue, such as defining the authority of a foreman in a department or settling the pay rate of a certain type of worker, it is exceedingly difficult to determine whether the decision is in fact a local issue or one which may have company-wide ramifications. The problem will be referred to again in terms of the whole issue of decision-making in the Japanese organization. At this point one should bear in mind the existence of the parallel plant and main office organizations.

At the level of department heads a distinctive feature of Japanese organization is highlighted. The 13 department heads in this company have a total of 19 deputy or assistant department managers. This proliferation of assistants and deputies with their seniors provides a total of 51 persons at the top level of management.

As in other Japanese firms the departments are divided into sections. The main office of this firm has a total of 29 sections, with 22 persons serving in the positions of deputy and assistant section chiefs. The final division of the main office organization is the branch, with 47 branches of the sections. Nearly one out of three of the employees in the main office has a formal title and formal position in the organization—despite the fact that a very considerable volume of clerical, statistical, and accounting work is carried on in the main office without the aid of the many machines and computers now common in most American firms.

To summarize, there are three main features of main office organization. First, the organization is elaborately and minutely divided

into separate, formally distinct groupings. Second, a very high proportion of persons hold formal positions and titles. Third, the complexity
of the organization is heightened by the presence of large numbers of
deputies and assistants to department and section chiefs.

The organization chart now leads to one of the factories, where
just under 3,000 persons are employed. It is a relatively new plant producing modern radio-communications equipment and is in no sense old
fashioned or representative of regressive trends in Japanese management.
On the contrary, it is considerably more progressive and modern than
many. Within the factory there is the same division of staff and line as
seen in the main office. The administrative and staff functions, however, do not have a parallel system in the factory or line organization.
The two are formally quite distinct.

Seventeen administrative units report directly to the plant manager,
his deputy, and two assistants. They include 5 departments, each headed
by a department manager, with a total of 7 deputy and assistant department managers. Under the departments there are 20 sections, with 15
assistant section chiefs. The sections in turn are divided into a total of
78 branches. In the staff organization 12 section heads and 7 deputy
chiefs report to the plant manager. These sections in turn are divided
into 35 branches. Thus in this plant there are 183 executive positions
above the level of foreman or general foreman, with four levels of
management above the foreman level.

In general, the ratio of the number of persons in one level of management to that in the next descending level is roughly one to three in
the large Japanese factory. That is, one president has reporting to him
2 or 3 managing directors who are superordinate to about 10 department
chiefs. Each department is divided into about three sections and these

in turn into three or four branches. Although the terminology for these several units differs from plant to plant, the general structure is similar. The one-to-three ratio of division generally prevails at the several levels of foremen, with at least two groups of first-line supervisors. The terminology here varies greatly, as does the definition of the position, its authority, and responsibility. The common pattern is a work group of perhaps 10 laborers led by a group leader, whose job corresponds roughly to the role of gang boss in some American operations. Although this position does not usually carry formal responsibilities, it does have a formal title and rank in some plants. In a factory employing some 4,500 laborers, approximately 450 men would hold the rank of group leader or foreman and about 150 men would rank as general foremen, each with two or three groups under him.

This, in barest outline, is the formal organization of a representative large Japanese firm. The ratio of employees in formally differentiated positions to general clerical and factory employees is about one to six. Leaving aside the assistant and deputy positions, from worker to president in this minimal scheme there are nine levels of rank, which must not, however, be conceived of as a continuous progression. The differentiation between shokuin and koin discussed earlier makes for sharp division and wide differentiation of personnel in background and status between the levels of branch chief and foreman.

It is this division between status and role at the branch chief level that introduces an important addendum to the scheme in the plant described here. In a number of plants studied, where the component of technical training was of particular importance to plant functioning, an intermediate post was introduced between foreman and branch chief. It is ordinarily filled by young college graduates who, as a result of the recruitment and personnel methods used, cannot be placed in first-line supervisory positions. As recent graduates from college, they are not sufficiently experienced or trained to assume management responsibility. At the same time, owing to their status when hired, they cannot be placed as workers. They are therefore assigned variously titled posts in which they act as technical assistants to general foremen.

The creation of these intermediate positions is a good example of the kinds of adjustments and accommodations forced on the Japanese organization by the nature of the worker–firm relationship and the conflicting demands of technology and interpersonal relations. An extreme example of this conflict is provided by the situation in a mine in Shikoku, which is part of a major metals–producing complex. The miners are recruited from the mountain villages near this isolated section of Shikoku Island. Operations in this mine were initiated in the seventeenth century, and several generations of many of the families have worked in the mine. The role of tradition, superstition, and local custom in the actual mining operations is very great, and the men can be effectively supervised only by foremen and leaders thoroughly familiar with these customs and traditions. The young college graduates who will manage the mine, however, are recruited from the universities of Tokyo by the main office and dispatched to the mine area for a period. Although technically competent, these men are totally unequipped for supervision in these special circumstances. For example, if a miner should break a dish at breakfast he will under no circumstances go into the mine that day, believing that to do so would be certain death. Locally trained supervisors understand and respect the belief; young graduates of Tokyo's giant universities are less likely to be sympathetic. To make the personnel procedures fit the realities of supervisory demands in the mine, the company has developed a system of having two persons fill each of the intermediate supervisory posts. One is an experienced man with years in the locality. The other is a young engineer who may or may not remain in the local work situation for his full career. He must at any rate leave the actual supervision of the miners to his partner.

There are many similar situations in Japan; this is merely an extreme example of a common problem. The company is caught between the quite theoretical training of the Japanese university and the social demands of recruitment in the Japanese factory which prevent the staffing of managerial positions from the ranks of the work force. The result is a makeshift expansion of the hierarchy and the creation of an essentially redundant position, its functions and responsibilities poorly defined and its utility in considerable doubt. What is perhaps most important to note in this situation is the fact that the requirements of efficiency and rationalization of the productive organization yield to the demands of the social context in which the factory operates.

The complex and highly differentiated organizational system of the Japanese factory is of particular importance in two respects. The first is the effect of the organizational system on the decision-making process in the Japanese firm, and the second is the relation of the formal organization to the careers of the individuals in the organization.

In no respect is the difference between the American and Japanese firm more striking and the relationship between the social systems of the two societies and their business organizations more clear than in the area of decision-making. The elaboration of the managerial hierarchy in the Japanese firm has been illustrated. What has not been emphasized is the extent to which these formally distinct and well-defined positions are indefinite and poorly defined functionally. The elaboration of the structure in itself virtually ensures a considerable overlapping of the authority of more than one person in any given area of action. The problem of the differentiation of home office and factory has already been noted. Staff and line functions are not clearly differentiated, and there is a wide use of deputies and assistants whose authority is ambiguous. Further, since the range of any given individual's authority is not well defined, there is a tendency to move decision-making responsibility up the line of command. The consequences of these factors in terms of decision-making are several. In the first place, nearly all decisions are worked out by groups of people in conference and discussion, a necessarily slow and cumbersome procedure. Second, communication is not well defined, and the levels of authority through which decisions must be transmitted are numerous. Third, and perhaps most significant, it becomes nearly impossible in this system to fix individual responsibility for decisions or for errors in decision-making.

To cite a mundane example of how decision-making works and what its effects are on the people in the system, the bonus payment problem obviously has a considerable potentiality for trouble in the factory. Since workers of any sort are apt to feel discriminated against on individually determined payments of this type, it would seem that the bonus might be a major source of grievance in the shop. Japanese managers maintained, and no evidence appeared to the contrary, that little or no difficulty resulted from the bonus. One might argue in part that the apparent lack of dissatisfaction stems from a general docility on the part of the Japanese worker. It seems more likely, however, to result from the system used in making the bonus payment decision. There is no one person against whom the worker can direct any dissatisfaction he might feel over the decision. The bonus payment—which varies but little from individual to individual—is decided not alone by the worker's foreman, nor by his branch chief, nor section chief, nor personnel department, but by all of these together with the final approval of the department chief. Should the worker feel some resentment it must be directed against all of these people, or, rather, against the company as a whole. And since he stands in a somewhat special relationship to the company, such resentment is neither easily mustered nor expressed.

This kind of approach to decision-making is not confined by any means to the bonus or wage problem, but is, instead, characteristic of all decision-making in these large firms. The advantages of such a system are considerable and appear to be rooted in Japanese custom. The tradition of family counsels, in which the entire family joins in reaching a decision about family problems, and of village counsels, where the village as a whole discusses and decides village problems, has been noted by students of Japanese history and society. The pattern has been attributed both to the close interpersonal relations obtaining within the limited Japanese group and to the special importance of maintaining status and prestige for the Japanese individual. According to this argument it is impossible to expose an individual to the hazard of direct individual responsibility for a decision. In practice, this approach to decision-making in the factory protects the individual's position in the plant. When a man must spend his entire career in one factory or company, it is important that his prestige and reputation and his relations with others retain their integrity. The decision-making system is admirably adapted to this end.

The system, however, has its difficulties, and clear ones, from the point of view of effective factory operations. It is a slow and cumbersome way to meet fast-changing market and labor conditions. From the point of view of Western organization it has the disadvantage of precluding the possibility of clearly fixing individual responsibility and of rapidly and efficiently correcting weak spots in the organization. The system clearly depends on the alternative goals. The Japanese choice is in the direction of the support and maintenance of interpersonal relations within the company at the expense of maximum efficiency. It is a choice which Western advisors, hopeful of rationalizing Japanese production methods, have special difficulty in appreciating.

The second area of special interest in an examination of the formal organization of the factory is the relationship between the organizational system and the careers of the employees. The organization comprises two distinct parts for the employee. The first is that portion of the hierarchy, accessible to graduates of the old-system higher primary schools and present-day middle schools, which extends from apprentices through workers and group leaders to foremen. These employees are koin; and the calculus of their careers is a separate matter from that of graduates of other levels of schools for whom there extends, at least in theory, the remainder of the organization to the topmost positions. In fact, career progress is more circumscribed for high school graduates than university graduates; but leaving this aside the careers of the better educated persons take in these upper ranks.

There seems no question that the elaboration of positions in the upper reaches of management is partly caused by the extreme difficulty encountered in attempting to demote or fire employees and the need to offer title and rank to compensate for the limited flexibility of the wage system. Recalling the discussion of recruitment and compensation,

it is clear that if an error is made in recruitment into the shokuin group
some internal mechanism must be available to minimize the error. If a
man is not an able factory hand he is not fired, but he can be shifted
to some routine and harmless position without damaging the firm.
Similarly, a man who enters the company from college cannot be de-
moted or fired. The need for some system of relatively harmless positions for the shokuin who prove incompetent appears to account for
some of the elaboration of positions and titles. It is necessary to find
a niche for a man of insufficient capacity where he can perform minor
functions without too greatly harming the over-all effectiveness of the
plant and without damaging the prestige of the individual.

In addition to providing a safety valve for errors in recruitment,
the multiplication of positions also makes it possible to reward individuals with tangible evidence of career progress within the confines of a
single firm. The problem became especially acute following the war
and during the period of postwar adjustments in those companies which
had considerably expanded their work force during the war. They found
themselves and still find themselves heavily overstaffed at the management level. To compensate for temporary losses of personnel to the
armed forces, recruitment into management ranks had continued during
the war, but both wartime and prewar personnel were entitled to positions following the end of the war. This fact alone made for a generous
staffing at the shokuin level. Later, although this kind of war-expanded
firm did cut back sharply its factory force during the 1949-1950 period,
it was not able proportionately to reduce its management staff. Finally,
the large company, while willing to cut off entirely the recruitment of
additional laborers at the present time, feels that it must continue to
recruit college graduates, at least in reduced numbers. The result of

these factors is the presence in most Japanese firms of a very large number of management and staff personnel proportionate to those in laboring and clerical positions.

The net effect has been to retard sharply career progress among company executives, particularly since the retirement age of 55 is seldom observed in the upper reaches of management. The positions of deputy and assistant managers of sections especially make it possible for the company to offer some career recognition to men who would not otherwise achieve the advancement to which their seniority entitles them.

Apart from the need to reward able individuals, the pressure to provide career recognition is a function of two very general considerations. It will be recalled that wage differentiation is limited, and a title and the appurtenances of formal office are of course an alternative to increased wages in rewarding employees. Parenthetically, too, it might be noted that where one firm (or military organization or government agency) employs many titles and ranks, firms and organizations working in relation to it must also use a similar range of titles to facilitate communication.

More important by far is the second consideration in the use of title and position as career reward—the part played by age and age-grading in the Japanese company. The relationship between age and rank is a very close one in the Japanese firm. It can be generaliy stated that it is not possible to promote a man to a rank where he will be in authority over persons substantially senior to himself. By the same token it is necessary to promote a man to some extent when he reaches a sufficient chronological age. (Of course, since workers do not move from one firm to another, length of service and age are directly connected.) This general rule about seniority and promotions is true in both broad groupings within the plant, among laborers as well as staff workers.

Thus, for example, a group leader in a plant will have at least 10 and the foreman of the group 20 years of service. Progression within the management hierarchy is no less regularized by age. Age will not ensure progress beyond a certain point, but its lack will ensure that a man does not progress until his allotted years are fulfilled. Thus a college graduate will not achieve branch-chief status until he is about 30 to 35 years of age. He will be 35 or 40 at his next promotion, perhaps 40 or 45 at the next, and will become a department chief as he nears 50. Not all will go so far, but age forces promotion within broad limits. No college graduate could remain without some rank indefinitely nor, conversely, of course, could he be promoted as superior to older men.

The importance of age-grading in the Japanese company was illustrated in the one firm where a job classification system was found to be in effect. (Job classification, in a large and well managed company, is an unusual device for a Japanese firm.) Five grades of workers were established: apprentice, worker, skilled worker third class and second class, and worker "high class." Further study revealed that this classification was solely a function of length of service, divided respectively into men with up to 3, 10, and 15 years of service, and, finally, the position of foreman, which in this plant requires 20 years of service.

Because of the overstaffing of shokuin in many plants, this general rule of governing promotion by length of service exerts continued pressure to have available positions that are at least formally higher in the company hierarchy. The deputy and assistant posts have been devised to meet this demand, but to say that these positions are therefore nonfunctional in plant operations is not to say that the men holding them have no authority. They represent, rather, a further division of authority and a further dilution of the decision-making function, which worsens the already present shortcomings of the Japanese organizational system.

This discussion of the relationships between the formal organization and the career of the employee is not meant to imply that informal factors play no part in careers or career opportunity. Some of the informal factors have been pointed out in foregoing sections. For example, nepotism plays a definite role in the basic recruitment process. In addition, the literature on Japanese society makes reference to a special kind of informal relationship, known as the <u>oyabun-kobun</u>, or parent-child relationship, that should be briefly considered here. It is an explicitly recognized set of reciprocal obligations between senior and junior that have been observed and delineated for certain kinds of Japanese work relationships. In the course of this study some attention was paid this kind of relationship. On the whole it appears justified to report that the <u>oyabun-kobun</u> relationship in its true form does not exist in the large firm. Certain kinds of industry, especially stevedoring and construction work, retain this form of organization, however, and it is a conspicuous feature of the considerable gambling and entertainment industry of Japan. Apart from these semi-legal and illegal areas, it is interesting to note that the relationship survives most strongly in those industries which, in the United States at least, are most heavily ridden with racketeering; and the system has real parallels to American racketeering. It does not seem accurate to describe the relationships between people in the large Japanese firm in these terms.

It is quite true to say that relations between younger and older, superior and subordinate individuals often have a heavy component of what we might call paternalism, which has close parallels to the father-son relationship. Thus, for example, the Japanese foreman feels responsible for the well-being of his workers, quite outside the work situation. Family problems, death in the worker's family, illness, quarrels between workers on a personal level, the well-being of the worker in the community—all of these have been in the past and even now are important parts of the foreman's responsibility. However, this is not the kind of formal and organized relationship that is implied in the oyabun-kobun terminology.

Looking at the present situation, and thinking in terms of management relations especially, a more important term than oyabun-kobun is the word batsu, or clique. In the discussion of recruitment procedures it was noted that groups of young men entering shokuin status together in a given year are recruited from a limited number of universities, which means in practice that a given age group on entry into the company's employ has had some previous interaction and intimacy. This intimacy from college years is maintained in the company by dinners, parties, and other informal activities. Further, a senior member of management, usually a graduate of the same university, will often become familiar with and associated with the careers of such a group of younger men. On the basis usually of common university experiences and background there develop in the large firms distinct cliques that play a very considerable though informal part in career progress and success. It is this factor that helps account for the frequency with which graduates of foreign universities have real career difficulties in Japanese firms.

The role of a senior member of management in these clique structures underlines the importance of such a person in the training system of the Japanese firm. The elaborate methods used in American firms to train employees at all levels for their jobs is in little evidence in the Japanese company. Training is largely a matter of on-the-job training, learning from seniors and superiors. Thus the new factory hand is placed in an apprenticeship system and his learning is derived only in small part through formal schooling. Job learning takes place in the shop and, remembering that the vocational school or commercial or industrial curriculum is not part of the Japanese school system, it is the responsibility of the senior worker to teach the new worker the methods of the plant. This situation is no less true of management. The absence of formal training operations in the Japanese firm adds to the close relations between worker and superior and increases the ties that knit the worker to the company in an essentially paternalistic relationship.

These ties, established within the sprawling formal organization, parallel closely the kind of relationship indicated in the small textile factory between the owner and his workers. While the size of the organization precludes the intimate knowledge of and interaction with superiors that is the central force in the operation of the small workshop, two types of relations which parallel the system of the small shop may be seen in the large firm. The first is the strong tie between the company and the worker described earlier, the life-time commitment of worker and firm to each other, and the elaborate system of extra-monetary obligations and rewards that have been developed in the large plant. The second is the intrafirm relationship between superior and subordinate developed in the clique system at the management level and in the apprentice-teacher and worker-foreman relationship in the factory itself.

To present fully the close parallels between the small Japanese factory and the large one in terms of social organization, it is necessary to move beyond the formal system and look at the role of the company in the worker's total life activity. The interpenetration of job with other social activities that is so striking in the small factory may be seen also in the largest Japanese factories. The large factory, like the small 20-worker operation, is an organization which has its involvements with the whole range of the worker's life, an involvement expected and accepted by the workers and one which bears on such important questions as the role of the trade union in the Japanese factory.

6

THE FACTORY'S PLACE IN THE EMPLOYEE'S WORLD

Both in the minds of the workers themselves and in the actual functioning of the factory system in Japan, the relationships between workers and their seniors, and workers and the company, cannot be described in the limited and relatively impersonal way characteristic of such relations in large Western plants. An illustration of the personal relationships within the Japanese factory was provided by the response of several categories of employees to a questionnaire designed to determine their feelings on a number of points. The statement that "A good foreman looks at his workers as a father does his children" elicited nearly the strongest agreement from all groups. It is assumed that such a statement would be greeted with derision, or strong distaste, by an American factory worker, but the average view of the Japanese workers ranged between "moderate agreement" and "strong agreement." Without placing too great dependence on these responses, they do indicate an essential difference in the quality of the worker-supervisor relationship.

Something of the nature of the further involvement and commitment of worker and company can be appreciated by examining the extent to which the company and its activities and programs penetrate the life of the worker far beyond the work situation itself. While he enters the company for his entire career and the system of reward and career progress is dependent in large degree on personal and noneconomic factors, the company also accepts responsibility and the worker expects a commitment far exceeding the specific demands of an economic organization.

At the most personal level of involvement, the close interconnection of the business firm with the details of the workers' lives may be seen in the problems that arise in the company housing facilities. It has been noted that most large Japanese firms provide company-built and subsidized housing for at least one-third of their work force, a proportion which tends to increase in rural factories. A metals-processing firm in Shikoku provides well over half of its workers with company housing. As is customary, the area is set apart from other private housing in the locality and all residents are company employees and their families. A particular problem arose here when the workers' wives grouped together in a financial cooperative, each member contributing a sum of money to a fund from which members could withdraw in turn substantial sums for the purchase of durable household goods and other items. Such a system is sorely needed where financial loans are exceedingly hard to come by and incomes are low, but the company now has a policy of discouraging cooperative worker financial groupings. Some wives, eager to purchase a washing machine or radio, withdrew funds heavily and ill-advisedly from the group bank. When several of the workers' wives were unable to make the requested repayment to the group fund, the other members turned to the personnel department of the company for recovery of the money. When called to the office, one of the husbands found his monthly paycheck reduced and his family budget reviewed. He then received some general advice

on the financial management of his affairs. The important point to note
is that wives, workers, and company were right to assume that the company, although it had no direct concern in the matter, would act in the
situation and, further, that all parties concerned would accept the company's intervention.

Many similar instances could be cited. For instance, a factory in
Honshu, which has a similar housing arrangement, is alert to a special
kind of problem that it frequently encounters. As in many of these housing areas the relations between people in the housing area have a most
immediate reaction on intrafactory relations. Although there is some
separation of housing by rank in the factory, foremen's wives and workers'
wives will sometimes live near each other. Relations have on occasion
become strained when the wife of a worker was able to make purchases,
wear clothing, or provide her children with music lessons—to mention
some specific cases—which were beyond the resources of the wife of a
neighboring foreman. This inappropriate rank order among the women
in the housing area affects the relations in the shop. In order to relieve
the strains caused in the factory by this kind of interfamily conflict,
the company has found it necessary periodically to move families to
different houses, trying to mask the reasons for the move.

In another company, management's most pressing problem from the
standpoint of personnel relations and morale was the inadequate schooling provided for the children of workers and managers in its factory in
the Hokkaido district. The importance of college entrance in Japan has
been noted. Inadequate school training will very nearly preclude a
successful career in later life for the child owing to his inability to
enter college. To help overcome the disadvantage of the rural and isolated location of its Hokkaido factory, the company found it necessary

to establish special schools to aid the education of its employees' children.

These problems of family finances, living standards, and education give an indication of the range of involvement of the company in the life of the worker. What is most interesting about these situations is that company action was not taken reluctantly or accepted grudgingly. Both management and workers assume it is the company's responsibility to involve itself in such matters and the workers' privilege and duty to receive such assistance and attention.

In the typical large firm the company's involvement goes well beyond even these matters. It is customary to provide a wide range of training, totally unrelated to the job situation, for employees and their families. Lessons in those skills appropriate to well-mannered young Japanese ladies, such as flower arranging, the classic dance, and cooking, are attended by well over 90 per cent of the women workers in many plants. Sex education and birth control instruction are also included in the curriculum in a number of large factories. Somewhat alarmed at changes in attitudes and behavior since the war's end, management now also provides the wives of workers with a wide range of classes in homemaking, family management, and Japanese arts.

Turning to another area of group activity, the company participates with the worker and his family in religious ceremonies. Nearly all large factories have a shrine on the grounds and give a day's holiday to celebrate the shrine festival. An indication of the depth of this worker-company participation is provided by the annual shrine ceremony of a large mine in Shikoku. It is held at the beginning of the year, and symbolizes the unity of management and worker and sanctions the factory's productive efforts for the new year. As in most Japanese firms, all activity ceases in the mine and smelter for the New Year's holiday. The representatives of the miners, senior workers in the company, carry a large piece of ore, the first production in the new year, from the mine, which is some kilometers up the mountain, to a shrine at the base. Management and workers join together in prayers and songs at the shrine, where the mine and the workers receive the blessings of the priests. Three days later this piece of ore is transported to the smelter where it initiates smelter operations for the year. The ceremony is an ancient one, and in its ritual is symbolized the close nexus of relation between all personnel of the company.

Looking back now to the small textile factory operated by Mr. Watanabe, despite the hundred-fold and more increase in numbers, when compared to the elaborate organization and complex technology that sets the large firm apart from its tiny companions in the Japanese economy, the distance does not appear to be so great. In large factories the managers cannot duplicate Mr. Watanabe's paternal and intimate knowledge of his young workers, and there is an increased remoteness and impersonalization from the close matrix of obligation and responsibility that holds the small textile plant together. Yet, looking to the large American plant in the other direction, there is more in common between the large and small Japanese units in the way in which people are related to each other and to the organization than in the American counterpart of the large Japanese factory.

Analogies must be used cautiously and can hardly demonstrate conclusions, but there is an inevitable analogy when trying to describe relations in the Japanese factory. Compared with the relatively impersonal and rationalized systems of production and organization of the large American corporation, the Japanese factory seems family-like in its relations.

It is family-like. When a man enters the large Japanese company it is for his entire life. Entrance is a function of personal qualities, background, and character. Membership is revocable only in extraordinary circumstances and with extraordinary difficulty. As in a family, the incompetent or inefficient member of the group is cared for, a place is found for him, and he is not expelled from the group because he is adjudged inadequate. Again, family-like, the most intimate kinds of behaviors are the proper province of concern and attention from the other members of the group. Fidelity and tenure bring the highest rewards, and, should the group encounter financial difficulty, it is expected that all members will suffer these difficulties together. Rewards of money and of material are secondary to the total success of the entire group. And, family-like, there is little recourse for the member of the group who has erred in his choice of group or who is mistreated by other members of the group.

The analogy is unsatisfactory, however. The family conveys notions of propriety and sanction not appropriate to a factory description; the analogy says nothing of the roots and causes of the kinds of relations so described. Furthermore, the analogy of family conveys a feeling of static organization, stability, and continuity that is quite inaccurate in describing the Japanese factory. The factory system is not static, nor are the relationships in its units entirely stable. The relationships which have been described are modal and generally characteristic. At the same time, however, there are areas and types of strain in this system, strains which will in all probability increase in the future and force changes in the organization of the Japanese factory.

Generally speaking, the modal attitudes and motives which appear to underlie the organizational system in the factory are traditional ones. The system itself and the men in top management who are instrumental

in shaping and directing that system are very much products of prewar
Japan. These men in top management, now in their fifties and sixties,
were born in a Japan overwhelmingly rural and only a few decades removed from its deep isolation from the larger world. The large firms
they head often trace their origins directly to feudal merchant families,
and the traditions and philosophy of these families remain an active and
real force in the management practice of the companies. Most of the
separate factories investigated during this study are the result of the
introduction of new products and methods into the parent company at
the beginning of the twentieth century. It might be added that, whatever the merits of the anti-monopoly laws promulgated during the Occupation years, their effectiveness has been rather less than complete and
the intimate relations between the several companies once forming an
industrial combination have been substantially revived—if indeed they
ever disappeared.

In short, the factory organization and its leaders are directly and
closely tied to a nonurban, prewar, traditional Japanese experience
and outlook. Leaving aside the impact of changes in world markets,
international relations, and technological methods on the factory organization as now constituted, there are, in terms of the people in the system, points of stress where the attitudes and expectations of the employees do not fit well the organizational methods and the attitudes and
expectations of top management.

The problem of the young university graduates from Japan's great
cities, who have only a remote understanding of the beliefs and customs of the rural employees of the company, has already been noted.
It is a single instance of a more general problem—the considerable and
seemingly increasing gap in background and experience between rural

and urban Japan. Many of the large factories are located in rather
isolated rural areas, and their labor force is locally recruited, for the
most part, by the personnel department of the local factory. The management group, however, is recruited by the company's main offices
in a large city; and the young members of management are urban trained
and oriented. The Japanese organizational structure obviously requires
a considerable and intimate mutual understanding between workers and
managers. Since such an understanding is only partly available under
the recruitment and promotion systems used in the large factories, in
many of the rural plants there is a considerable gap between management and labor, with an apparently diminishing interaction and amount
of understanding between them.

Looking at the large factories in the cities, there is further evidence of the differences between rural and urban workers and the problems presented by these differences. It was pointed out that large factories would much rather confine their recruiting of permanent employees
to young men and women born and raised in the country. Their "nature,"
it is said, is "more stable." In this statement stability apparently refers
to the extent to which the worker can accept without dissatisfaction or
unrest the working conditions and relations in the plant. Enthusiasm
for union membership is only one, but an important, example of the
lack of stability in city-raised employees.

There seems to be in these types of tensions a broad area of stress
between the structure of the organization and its personnel. Exposed
to and affected by the many changes that have taken place in Japan
at an accelerated pace in the past two decades, young, urban-trained
persons do not fit comfortably into the system as it has been maintained.
Dissatisfaction with the age-dominated approach to career advance-

ment is marked and freely expressed by many younger men in management. Impatience with the wage system, both for its heavy component
of nonfinancial recompense and for the weighting it gives to age and
seniority, is evident among the younger employees. Management feels
strongly that the ever-increasing pool of city-trained workers does not
fit the system of relations now employed in the factory. This sentiment
finds expression in both the training programs designed to inculcate
traditional values and the recruiting procedures employed.

There is no more striking instance of the kind of tension and other
strains caused by the lag between changes in the broader society and
the present factory system than the role of women in the Japanese company. Perhaps more than in any other single area of interaction, the
relations between men and women in Japan contrast sharply with those
which have developed in the West. More perhaps than any other type
of interaction, changes induced or accelerated by events of recent
years have affected the role, attitudes, and behavior of Japanese
women. The resulting tension is highly visible in the factories and
offices of the large Japanese companies.

It is difficult to observe any accommodation of the policies or attitudes of the companies to changes in the broader social position of
women. It is the firm and hard-held conviction of men in all parts of
the companies—the personnel departments no less than others—that
women employees will remain and should remain in the company's employ only until they are married, and that this marriage should properly
take place at an age no later than thirty years. Mr. Watanabe in his
small factory is in a position to actively ensure the marriage of his employees, either by aiding its arrangement or by himself arranging the
marriage. In larger firms there is considerable pressure on women em-

ployees to leave the firm after they have worked for the company for some ten years, and the pressure is substantially increased by the fact that almost without exception the women employees will have no chance whatsoever to improve their job status in the company.

This problem of job status is not only a matter of performing jobs at the lowest level of competence or responsibility but also involves such less formal reinforcements of differential status as the preparing and serving of tea to male visitors to the office, the running of errands at the request of fellow employees, and the performance of other routine or even menial tasks. The only exceptions to these general rules governing the employment and the job role of women in the company occur in those plants which employ a large proportion of women. They will sometimes become group leaders in shops employing only women, and on very rare occasions become foremen. No instance of a woman in a titled or responsible position was encountered in the shokuin ranks.

It may be that at some earlier period in Japan's history the assignment to women of only routine, menial tasks was accepted by them as inevitable and proper. Some women employees appear to accept this role without difficulty. It is clearly not true to state that all women accept their job position passively and happily at present. A very great increase in the number of women graduates of colleges and universities has been made possible in the postwar period. The proportion of women seeking careers in business, laboratories, and other professional jobs has gone up sharply. In one company, where the problem of the woman's role was looked at rather closely (a company quite westernized in its general approach to personnel problems), a number of women's college graduates have been hired since the war. They appear, to an outsider at least, to be outspokenly unhappy and even bitter at their position in the company. The company's response to the situation has been to curtail entirely the hiring of women college graduates and to confine its recruitment of female employees to high school and middle school graduates.

The situation has obvious similarities to that in the West in the first decades of the twentieth century. A possible difference is the emphatic and seemingly unanimous rejection by the men in these companies of any suggestion that women might usefully and advantageously be employed in responsible positions by the firm. To support the company's position references are made to the underemployment of Japanese men and the supposed inherent instability of women as employees.

An examination of the role of women in the large Japanese firm reveals something of both the kind of problems which social change and changes in the attitudes of employees are creating for the companies and the customary response of the companies to these problems. There is a very strong conservatism in these matters, and the characteristic response to this kind of problem is one of denial or avoidance. But the pattern of interpersonal relations appropriate to the factory as it is now organized, the intimacy between worker and supervisor, the dependence of worker on the firm, and the immobility of the employee—all are subject to strain as a result of changes in the background and thinking of the younger and urban-bred employees. It is a strain that seems likely to increase.

Against this background of the visible stresses in the relation between company and employee, it is possible to discuss more effectively the question of unions and union membership. Without underestimating the potential importance of unions in Japanese factory relations or the importance they have at present in the minds of the workers as a good and necessary part of the work setting, the absence of union influence and the paucity of discussion on union relations when interviewing in and observing the factory situations was a striking and disturbing fact. As they are presently organized, Japanese labor unions, of course, are almost entirely a product of the postwar period. They enjoyed an explosive growth in the early days of the Occupation, and every large plant is union organized, has a union shop system, and a contract with a union. The most casual observer of the Japanese political scene must be impressed with the very considerable and impressive strength of the unions, a strength which appears to be increasing.

However, when one observes not the Tokyo headquarters, the political scene, or the histories and statistics relating to the union movement in Japan but the actual workplaces themselves, the union does not appear to be an important factor in the day-to-day job relations of the worker—in his relations with the foreman, in his interaction with company officials, or in his activities in the housing area or community outside the plant. The position of the union in Japanese factories is, of course, particularly striking when seen in contrast to the role played by the union in large American plants, where the settlement or avoidance of grievances indicates the importance of the union in the shop and where discussions on matters of factory relations with personnel department members, foremen, workers, or managers will, if carried on to any extent, inevitably touch on or center upon the union and its relations with management.

To give an example of the differences, no Japanese company was encountered where an equivalent of the grievance procedures common in American companies was in actual effect. Unlike the American contract, the union contract in Japan, although often lengthy, does not deal with the details of the actual working relations—defining the foreman's role, setting out the relations between supervisor and worker, and circumscribing the role of management in its operations. Further, while contractual in form, the union agreement does not have the legalistic implications of the American contract. Its terms deal primarily with agreement on the existence of the union, its relations with the workers, and on wages and hours. It is a flexible document, indeed. In some companies it is subject to quarterly review, which, in effect, means that wages, the primary concern of the agreement, are under continual negotiation. The bonus payment, which is negotiated semi-annually, also provides a periodic crisis in union relations. In conversations with the men in management there was no indication of a real or deep concern over the union's present or potential strength in the shop. Given the surplus of labor in Japan and the brief history, erratic leadership, and tenuous role of the unions in the actual workshop, management does not seem to see the local union as a real threat to its essentially autonomous functioning.

At the same time it would be incorrect to state that the average factory worker is indifferent to or unaware of the labor union. The responses to questionnaire items dealing with labor unions revealed quite general feelings that unions are necessary, not too powerful at present, and that they must be continued at least at their present level of strength.

The uncertain and limited role of the union in the actual workplace seems to derive from two factors: first, the history and leadership of the union and, second, the relationship between worker and company, which, so long as it is successfully maintained, allows little scope for an active local union. This study was not concerned with Japanese labor unions except as they appeared to be a factor in the local factory situation. For detailed and thorough reviews of the Japanese trade union movement reference should be made to the several historical studies available.

Looking only at the local situation, an indication of the inexperience of union leadership is gained from the history of the first postwar negotiation in a single factory. During the liberal atmosphere of the 1920's, this plant had an independent trade union. Although opposed first by a company union and later by increasingly nationalistic and rightist company-supported organizations, it survived until the depression days of 1931. No independent union existed from that time until the immediate postwar period when Japan became aware of the positive attitude of the Occupation authorities toward labor unions. With the promulgation of the Occupation directives governing labor unions, local organizations and national union groups appeared. The management of this plant became aware of the existence of a local group when three representatives of the local called on the factory manager early on New Year's Day, 1946. The union men presented three demands: first, that democratic practices be initiated In the plant; second, that the union be recognized; and, third, that wages in the plant be doubled. Since the first demand was sufficiently general and the second sufficiently reasonable, under the circumstances they presented no difficulties for agreement. The third, an immediate two-fold increase in wages was another matter. Agreement was finally reached on a 20 per cent increase, management reporting that this was apparently a palatable solution because the Japanese word for two times, nibai, is similar to the word for 20 per cent, _niwari_. Management at least claims that the similarity was sufficient to allow the union leaders to retreat from the excessive enthusiasm of their first demand. Whatever the merits of this story, the abruptness of union development and the absence of a leadership with experience and training are illustrated by the anecdote. Although some number of nationally known individuals could be and were mustered to direct trade unions in terms of national policy and politics, there seems not yet to have appeared in local unions the kind of experienced and dedicated leadership necessary to solidify its position in the local work situation.

Regardless of the leadership available, however, there is little room in the customary system of relations in the large Japanese factory for a strong local union, that is, apart from the wage problem. The wretched wages paid in many industries and factories have led to some spectacular and bitter strikes in the postwar period to raise the wage level. In those plants observed where the wage level was at least the national average, there appeared to be a very slight connection between rank-and-file union membership and the large national union. Further, it might be noted that in the factories of the large firms with a standard pay level it is fairly common for the unions at each of the company's several plants to group together in a single organization not otherwise affiliated with a labor organization. Insofar as the gap between management and the workers, as, for example, the difference in background and training between newly hired _koin_ and _shokuin_, continues to increase, it appears that the union will come to play an important part in the local situation. In the Japanese system as now constituted, there is little room for a union when the system is functioning effectively. The loyalty the system compels and the intimacy of the system leave little room for allegiance to still a third party in the actual workplace. The workers in the large firms see the union as a potential counterbalance to the excessive employment by management of its prerogatives. When seen from the point of view of the local work situation, the position of the national trade union in Japan appears not unlike that of the federal government in the United States—a third party in the work situation, not properly active but essentially friendly to the workers and a force necessary to curb the free play of management's actions.

In considering the potential of the union in the local situation a further point should be made. Although the weakness at the local level may be caused by the lack of effective leadership, the promotion system now in general use in the factories may well make such leadership available to the unions in the future. As a general rule, with but very few and conspicuous exceptions, ambitious young men who are sons of a laborer or farmer and educated only to the middle school level have no chance to realize their ambitions in the employ of the company. It appears likely that such young men will look to a career in the union, or a political career with union support, as a channel for their hopes and ambitions. Not only does management deprive itself of able leaders by its policies of recruitment and promotion but also it may supply antagonistic leadership to the local union.

7

CONTINUITY AND CHANGE IN JAPANESE INDUSTRY

One of the ultimate tests by which to measure the success or lack of success of the functioning of an industrial organization is the productivity of the units of the system. This study has not been directly concerned with the physical equipment, technology, or products of the factories of Japan or with the capital expenditures and revenues of the companies observed. Nevertheless, the existence of the intimate connection between social organization and productivity and the special concern attaching at present to problems of productivity seems to warrant some special consideration of the problems involved in raising the productivity levels in the large Japanese factory.

Productivity is, of course, a relative measurement, and the standard customarily used by Japanese executives is that of the output and cost of production of an American factory. By and large, Japanese executives are not flattering to their companies when they make such a comparison. Estimates are necessarily rough, and it would be difficult and misleading to attempt to derive an exact value. However, in comparing their plants with American factories producing similar items, few Japanese executives would venture a productivity proportion as high as 50 per cent of a comparable American unit, and a more frequent estimate is one-sixth to one-fifth of the productivity of their American counterparts. American observers have estimated a ratio of one-fifth, that is, the productivity of Japanese factories is about 20 per cent of that in a comparable American plant. One plant, using American processes and machines to produce a product under American patents and thus identical in factory setup to the American firm, was reported by the manager to produce at a rate of about 60 to 70 per cent of the American company. This was the highest percentage reported by any plant observed.

Although there is a real basis for doubting that such numerical comparisons can be made for a large number of factory units, these kinds of estimates point to a real problem, and one that provides an opportunity to examine the effects of social organization on the actual operations of the factory. Solutions to the problems of increasing productivity and the analysis of factors which tend to depress productivity are usually made in terms of engineering and technical factors and changes in the factory's technological organization. Without minimizing the importance of these aspects of productivity and their role in increasing output, the possibility remains that a good part of the problem in Japan may be attributable not so much to technical factors as to the effects of the social organization on the productivity system.

These remarks, critical both of the level of productivity and of technological change, are made in the face of the fact that Japan has over the past decade, when the nation's output is taken in the large, staged an astonishing advance in output, achieved a considerable increase in productivity, and introduced a large amount of the latest technology. This discussion of productivity and technological change, however, is focused on the existing plant, where machines, a work force, a managerial group, and a system of production are already in

operation. It is within these existing facilities that the problem assumes the shape described here. On the basis of the observations made,
large companies seem to introduce new technical systems by the establishment of entirely new plants in new locations, largely employing a
new and separate labor force.

Productivity might be defined as the balance between factory output and the cost of producing that output. This cost may include materials, labor, capital expenditure, equipment, supply, research, and
marketing. In considering the cost-output equation and attempting to
solve it for Japan, there is an important difficulty, namely, the relative role of labor and machines in the Japanese and American systems
of production. Japanese businessmen, no less than American specialists, are prone to accept the form of the equation as derived for American production. This makes for a somewhat misleading comparison.
Since labor is the most considerable cost in American production, to
minimize production costs and maximize productivity the amount of
and effective utilization of machine equipment and methods becomes
the key to maximized productivity. This is not the situation in the
Japanese factory, where machinery represents the most considerable
cost and, relative to both machine cost and the American situation,
of course, labor cost is very low. This comparison is relevant to a
wide number of factors in productivity. For example, the use of hand
labor and hand-propelled carts would by American standards be a most
expensive and inefficient system of transporting materials and semi-
finished goods within the factory. It is not nearly so luxurious an expenditure where labor costs are so low.

More important than this problem of seemingly wasted labor—by
American standards—and further complicating a direct comparison of

productivity in the two systems, is the fact that fixed costs in Japan
are not confined to such items as inventory and equipment. Labor, too,
in Japan represents a fixed cost, one not susceptible to adjustment as
conditions require. The no-layoff, no-firing rule has been described.
In terms of productivity it means that a very large labor force, fixed
in size and cost, will be maintained. The problem for management is
not one of reducing the amount of labor required in production but,
rather, to maximize the amount of labor required in order to be able to
actively employ the entire work force and proportionately reduce the
amount of investment in equipment, power, and space.

There is thus a basic difference in the relative role of equipment
and labor in the two economies that makes these comparisons misleading. Nevertheless, whatever figure is assigned to these factors and
whatever productivity estimate is finally derived for Japan, it would
seem accurate to maintain that productivity in Japan is substantially
below the American average. This low productivity is a result in large
part of the different social organizations; and Western-inspired technological changes can have only a limited effect on the productivity level
and, indeed, can in some respects only aggravate the problem.

More than any other single factor affecting productivity at present
is the general rule, traditional and strong, that employees at all levels
of the company have a permanent position with the company. Most
Japanese firms have a labor surplus on the payroll, and it is no less
evident at the management level than in the shop. The proliferation
of make-work jobs and the use of labor-saturated methods in production are in large part a result of this. More important, the presence of
a labor surplus effectively blocks off much incentive to improve methods of production. For example, labor-saving machinery can hardly

be considered beneficial by management when the displacement of labor costs by the machine simply compels management to add that labor
cost to some other part of the total operation. Systems of management
and production which reduce the labor requirement become actually
harmful in the Japanese factory. For instance, Japanese offices are
heavily staffed with clerical workers doing the most elementary accounting and statistical operations by hand. Apart from the question
of whether machines of the IBM type would represent a saving in terms
of Japanese labor costs, the displacement of this clerical force by machines would not, at least in the short run, represent an over-all saving. Whether the machine costs were paid in salaries or in the special
retirement allowances paid at severance they would be additional to
present labor costs. Not included in this consideration is the undoubted
damage to morale of such displacement.

The general organization principle of permanent employment also
affects productivity in terms of the efficient use of present personnel.
First of all, the extreme difficulty in ridding the firm of inefficient
employees further exacerbates the make-work problem of finding harmless positions for persons in management or the shop who have been
proved inadequate. Second, a substantial threat to the work force is
removed and, by Western notions at least, a major incentive to steady
and effective production is taken away. Despite the absence of a
threat of firing, it does not seem justified to argue that the Japanese
laborer is less energetic in his job performance than his Western counterpart. However, his present energies are compelled by such matters
as loyalty to the firm and close relations with his immediate supervisors.
These motivations to job effectiveness would be removed if the impersonal job relationship of the West were substituted for the present system.

Thus changing the present basis of employment for what the West would see as a more rational one would require the most far-reaching changes in the incentive system—if, indeed, such changes would be appropriate to the psychology of the Japanese worker.

The immobility of the work force in the factory means not only that management cannot manipulate its labor force to serve as a part of the productivity equation but also that workers at all levels who are dissatisfied with their jobs have great difficulty in changing them. This factor, too, has its effects on over-all productivity. The labor immobility problem has been discussed only in terms of the local factory. It is likely that its broad economic effects are most keenly felt and observable when the entire economy is viewed as a single unit.

Closely related to the permanent employment rule in its effects on productivity is the influence of the recruitment system employed by the large Japanese firm. Since placement of new employees is largely on the basis of jobs open at the time of employment, competence for a particular job—apart from general professional training for technical positions—is not a factor in the selection process. This is in sharp contrast to the Western practice of basing employment and selection on the appropriateness of the individual's skills and experience for a specified position. The most effective placement and the most productive use of personnel undoubtedly require rather careful fitting together of position and person, as well as the ability to easily move people from one position to another in the event that the fit of person and position is not a good one. In these respects the Japanese firm is considerably handicapped by its present practice, but it must be emphasized that the Japanese method is neither capricious nor the result of inadequate understanding of personnel methods. Rather, the approach to selection is a close-knit part of the whole approach to personnel problems.

A similar situation is encountered when examining the Japanese approach to promoting people in the shop and office. There can be no question that promotions so heavily, indeed almost exclusively, governed by age and seniority are costly to efficiency. Although the promotion problem also involves such matters as the lack of job classification and evaluation which make it difficult to single out rational factors on which to base promotions, it comes down to the fact that age and seniority are important in all aspects of life in Japan. The factory will and must conform to the broader social usage.

As with promotions, so with pay. The entire system of reward and recompense rises out of and forms part of a pattern with social custom. The distance between the manorial lord in a nonmonetary economy exchanging services with his followers and the Japanese firm using wages as only a part of the exchange of obligations with its workers is not great. From the point of view of efficiency it makes no sense whatsoever that two men doing identical work side by side should, by reason of size of family, age, or some other consideration irrelevant to their work output, receive wholly different rewards. In terms of efficiency it is also illogical to have a skilled worker receive a good deal less pay than an unskilled worker. Yet it is assumed that it is proper and fitting that a young man who is responsible only for his own living expenses, and indeed probably still subsidized by his family, should receive substantially less pay than a man with a wife and children to support and the other demands of maturity pressing hard on him.

The Japanese pay system removes from the work setting the use of money as a primary incentive for higher individual productivity. This affects the application of piece-work systems, close cost analysis, job specification and evaluation procedures, and other methods of increasing productivity commonly applied in the West. Much of this apparatus is based on the pay system and its incentives and punishments. The application of these methods in the large Japanese factory is extremely difficult.

A good part of the problem of pay systems and incentive methods rests on the effort to avoid assigning individual responsibility or blame in the Japanese group, thus waiving the question of individual reward or punishment. This underlying philosophy in the organization has repercussions on company efficiency at several points. A minor example of its effects is provided by the kind of inspection or quality control carried out. In a factory producing steel tubing the management had a considerable problem of low-quality output. The tubing produced was for oil-well operations for export markets and had to meet rather exacting inspection standards. The tubing was given 100 per cent inspection at three points in its production, an extremely costly procedure. At final inspection the rejection rate was still high. Such problems of quality control are not unknown in American firms. What was most striking in this factory was the fact that the problem was at no time communicated to the workers. The engineering group was in charge of the quality of output, but the workers were not informed of the problem and no effort was made either to assign blame to individuals for the situation or to arouse on the part of the workers an effort to improve the quality. There is no doubt that this particular situation was in part the result of the generally poor level of communication between management and workers. A more important influence, however, was the customary avoidance of fixing on particular persons the responsibility for errors or failure in production. At a more general level, the cumbersome system of making, communicating, and enforcing management decisions and the proliferation of management positions are instances of this same attitude. Authority is not well defined and responsbility is not easily assigned.

There is another general feature of the Japanese firm, which has not yet been discussed, that is relevant to this review of the ways in which the nontechnical aspects of organization affect productivity. To make the contrast between Japan and the West clear, a brief summary of the American approach might be made. On entering an American firm to discuss the organization's activities and problems, the job of one of the first persons encountered, and probably the first problem cited—overriding production, labor relations, and other areas of concern—is that of company sales. Senior personnel will often have sales backgrounds; a substantial part of the staff of the company will be in sales work. Sales and marketing problems, advertising methods, the development of new products and markets—all are a constant part of the thinking of men at all levels of the company and are of continuing concern. It is a philosophy of expansion and change.

In marked contrast, one can spend many days discussing company policy and problems in the large Japanese firm at all levels of the company and, except for a possible concern that orders are insufficient, hear nothing at all about sales, marketing, or advertising. There is a clear relationship between the roots of this apparent lack of concern for sales and the productivity problems. For example, the local Japanese market is generally assumed to be a limited one offering but little opportunity to the company. Whether this assumption is in fact correct is certainly questionable. In most lines of production, however, there is little taste for engaging in direct competition for a larger share of the present domestic market; that is, for directly attacking the market and other companies by appealing to the consumer. Further, interest in and investment in the development of new products is low.

Whether cause or effect, the usual Japanese practice has been to have sales and distribution in the hands of a third party—a trading firm or jobber. Although it is true that the trading company will usually be closely allied with the main office of the firm, the factory itself is usually insulated from direct concern with sales. The typical prewar cartel had as its central unit a trading company which acted on behalf of the entire grouping of manufacturing units. This lack of attention in the manufacturing firm to sales and marketing, and lack of experience in the fields, is the most conspicuous symptom of a general conservatism of Japanese management in relation to company operations. Leaving aside the political conservatism which is itself an overriding feature of management's attitudes, there is a general desire on management's part to hold on to present markets, to operate within the present framework, and, generally, to maintain rather than expand. In terms of productivity, this underlying philosophy of the men in management further reduces the possibility of demands that might be present in the system to change procedures or to increase productivity.

To point to some of these procedures and attitudes as illustrative of the effects of the organizational system in depressing productivity is not to say that the system is a bad one or that another might be substituted to increase productivity. Indeed, it might be argued that it is only with this organizational system that large-scale productivity in

Japan was and is possible at all. In considering productivity and organization what is important is the manner in which technological methods and problems are rooted in social and attitudinal aspects of Japanese society. Change in one area of the total factory complex will involve changes in a whole series of areas, changes that will not necessarily have a positive total effect.

In connection with the statement that change in one part of the factory system reverberates beyond the point of change and can be positive and successful in effect only if seen in terms of the total system, the present efforts of Western technicians in Japan—Americans especially —might be noted. Owing to both a long experience in looking to other nations for ideas and methods in industry and the present American view that Japan's industrial success is important to American political success, a considerable effort is being made by Americans to stimulate productivity in Japan. Given what are to the eyes of an engineer or technician glaring and obvious inadequacies in the Japanese production methods, suggestions and recommendations for changes are freely offered to the Japanese. Further, seeing the success of American methods in the American setting, there is no small readiness on the part of many Japanese to study and attempt to institute American production methods. Some of the ways in which the abrupt and piecemeal imposition of American technology in Japan is interferred with, prevented, or meets with unfortunate results are evident from this study.

At the present time it would seem that the greatest need in the Japanese factory is for methods of production which are generally the converse of the American in their effects. American production methods are increasingly designed to minimize the labor component and to impersonalize and rationalize the organization; the Japanese need is for a production system which can make the greatest use of labor within a personalized system of relations. Such a system might be devised and such changes developed, but the necessary changes cannot be developed in the American setting. They can only be developed in a factory system like that of Japan. Instead of the brief flying trip of Japanese experts to American plants or the short-term advice of American consultants in Japan, it seems that it would be beneficial to the Japanese factory to have trained advisors, regardless of nationality, committed to a considerable period of work in one factory. They could learn the factory's organization and methods and later assist in developing solutions to productivity problems. Thus, rather than the occasional consultant or technical advisor, there would be advisors who had become part of the system. Then, thoroughly familiar with local practice and needs and working within the system, they could help set up devices and methods appropriate to the system of production now employed in the large Japanese factory.

8

PRODUCTIVITY IN THE JAPANESE FACTORY

Thus far efforts to promote industrialization in non-Western societies have been devoted largely to problems of assistance and change in the areas of finance and technology. The results of these efforts have drawn attention to the importance of social organization and of patterns of social interaction to the process of economic change, and emphasize the need for a further understanding of the interaction between technology and human relations for effective economic development.

Japan's extraordinary history of industrialization remains a unique record of effective social change, compelling the attention of those concerned with problems of industrialization and economic development in non-Western societies. Japan strode from hard-held Asian insularity to a central role in world industry, world trade, and world power relations in a single, explosive burst of energy and remains the singular case of non-Western industrialization. The outlines of the story are familiar; its implications for present attempts effectively to bring about development in other countries are evident.

Yet there are gaps in available knowledge of the process as it took place in Japan, areas in which evidence on critical issues in Japan's transition is inadequate or contradictory. What particular changes were central to the transition; what elements of the total structure

changed; what drives and needs made it possible for Japan to utilize
the knowledge and skills of the West where other nations could or did
not; and what kinds of people were the leaders, the men who turned
away from traditional modes and directed the changes? It is in the
answers to these questions that helpful insights might be found for present work in other societies.

The general view of Japan's economic transition is that the changes
in Japanese society were revolutionary and entire. Far from being confined to those more superficial matters of habit, dress, and taste that
peoples customarily find rather easy to adjust, they are held to have
cut deep into the very roots of the nation's social system. Levy states,
for example, that:

> The changes were revolutionary as far as the social structure of
> the society was concerned, and industrialization of a marked
> degree, far beyond anyone's expectations in the West, was
> achieved in a very short time. It is perhaps doubtful that any
> society ever carried out such marked changes so quickly and
> with so little violence. Land tenure, education, production
> and consumption systems, political systems—virtually every-
> thing—either changed or had its position in the total structure
> changed radically. [1]

What impressed observers of the transition in Japan was more than the
extensive effects and the great speed of change. Germany too had
moved toward a thorough industrialization very rapidly not long before
Japan's singular adventure was undertaken. Germany, however, is of
the West, the very birthplace of those attitudes and actions held to be
an essential part of the process, as, for example, the Protestant world

---

[1] Marion J. Levy, Jr., "Contrasting Factors in the Modernization of China and
Japan," in Economic Growth: Brazil, India, Japan, ed. by Simon Kuznets,
Wilbert E. Moore, and Joseph J. Spengler (Durham: Duke University Press, 1955),
pp. 532-533.

view. Japan's transition began from what was in most respects a greatly different historical and social setting. It then seemed that, in order to accomplish an effective and lasting transition, Japan would need to change rapidly in respects other than technology. As early as 1915, in characteristic turn of phrase, Thorstein Veblen stated the general implications of this picture of revolutionary technological change for social relationships and for attitudes and motives of the Japanese.

> It should, then, confidently be presumed that, as Japan has with great facility and effect taken over the occidental state of the industrial arts, so should its population be due, presently and expeditiously, to fall in with the peculiar habits of thought that make the faults and qualities of the western culture—the spiritual outlook and the principles of conduct and ethical values that have been induced by the exacting discipline of this same state of the industrial arts among the technologically more advanced and mature of the western peoples.[2]

In the interval since Veblen's presumption, the view of a close and even necessary connection between certain kinds of social systems and industrialization has been much strengthened. A series of polarities have been put forth to indicate the directions of social change, change in attitudes and social interaction, upon which change to an industrial society is held to depend. Each describes an element of a general shift in the basis of social interaction assumed necessary to the change from a preindustrial to an industrial society. The view that the outcome of industrialization would be parallel for the social system of Japan and that of the West is set forth in Lockwood's careful study of Japanese economic development:

---

[2]Thorstein Veblen, "The Opportunity of Japan," in Essays in Our Changing Order, ed. by Leon Ardzrooni (New York: The Viking Press, 1943), p. 254.

In the traditional East, as formerly in the West, the Industrial
Revolution requires a revolution in social and political arrange-
ments no less than in production technology. Steam and steel,
joint-stock finance, and laboratory science can transform the
economic life of any backward area. Yet they are only tools
at best. Their successful application necessitates a whole pattern of pervasive, interlocking changes in traditional societies.
They can only be put to work within a new social setting which
entails a radical break with the past, led by new elements in
the society who will reject the sanctity of old ways and understand the social prerequisites of the new technology.[3]

These propositions argue that economic development, in Japan and

elsewhere, is dependent on a series of changes quite outside the area

of finance and technology, changes in at least two broad sectors of

the society. First, an issue susceptible of historical examination, the

process will require a group of leaders from outside the strata that pro-

duced preindustrial leadership. Second, effective economic develop-

ment will be accompanied by profound changes in the social structure,

changes eventuating in patterns of interaction quite like those evolved

in the West through the Industrial Revolution.

On the first of these issues, that of the leadership of Japan's indus-

trialization, opinions differ. Central roles in the leadership of politics

and industry during Japan's transition have been assigned those lesser

nobility who under the feudal regime suffered a loss of economic status

and who held but little power or influence before the transition period.[4]

Again, the merchants of Japan, enjoying great wealth but deprived by

[3]William W. Lockwood, The Economic Development of Japan, Growth and
Structural Change, 1868-1938 (Princeton: Princeton University Press, 1954),
p. 499.

[4]George B. Sansom, The Western World and Japan, A Study in the Interaction of European and Asiatic Cultures (New York: Alfred A. Knopf, 1950).

feudal law of commensurate social status, have been seen as central figures in the changes.[5] A recent study of the early period of change assigns an important role to the peasants.[6] Still another view has lately been offered:

> The ease with which the transition was accomplished owes much not only to vigorous and imaginative leadership, but also to the fact that the political revolution represented merely a re-distribution of power within the governing class rather than an upheaval destructive of the old society. Consequently Japan carried into the new era traditional sentiments and loyalties which permitted her to undergo immense material changes without the loss of social cohesion. Even high officials of the Shogunate did not usually feel themselves precluded, on the overthrow of the old order, from serving under the new Imperial regime, which was thus able to recruit many able bureaucrats trained in the business of government.[7]

There is then an unresolved question concerning the kinds of people who led the Japanese move to industrialization, their social origins, and whether in fact the change in leadership through this period was revolutionary in nature. The proposition that these new elements of leadership represented a break with the past might better be restated to indicate the underlying continuity that accompanied alterations in elite groups. It would be of considerable interest in terms of understanding Japan's experience, and of some importance to the better understanding of the process of change in other nations, to have available a thorough analysis of this leadership group in Japan.

[5]Levy, op.cit.

[6]Thomas C. Smith, Political Change and Industrial Development in Japan: Government Enterprise, 1868-1880 (Stanford: Stanford University Press, 1955).

[7]G. C. Allen, and Audrey G. Donnithorne, Western Enterprise in Far Eastern Development (New York: The Macmillan Company, 1954), p. 188. (This quotation has been used with the permission of the Macmillan Company.)

Of more fundamental importance than the question of leadership of the transition is that concerning the degree of continuity or discontinuity in social structure and systems of social interaction from the pre-industrial society to industrialization. The assumption is that industrial development on the Western model requires a social setting radically different in nature from preindustrial relationships, a system fundamentally akin to that which developed in the West. The problem is no less complex than it is important. It would be presumptuous, with the limited knowledge of Japan's social system now available, to state the answer for the Japanese case to the general proposition. Still the results of this study of the large Japanese factory bear on this issue.

It might be assumed that, more than any other institution, the large manufacturing plant would represent in its social organization the extreme accommodation of Japanese systems of organization to the demands of industrial technology. Differences in organization, retaining similarities to earlier forms, might persist in rural social groupings and not be directly relevant to this question of the connections between social change and economic change. However, such lags in adaptation would presumably be minimized in the large factory.

In the foregoing chapters a general examination of several areas of the organization of the large Japanese factory has been undertaken. The areas dealt with and the detail of the study are hardly exhaustive; it may still be possible on their review broadly to make out differences between the usual American factory organization and that common in the large factories of Japan, and to make some general statement of the nature of the differences. Leaving aside exceptions and details, some general features of the Japanese organization might be summarized.

1. Membership in the Japanese productive group is a permanent and irrevocable membership. Workers at all levels of the factory customarily work in but one company. They spend their entire career in that single firm which is entered immediately on completing their education. The firm will continue to provide the worker's income at whatever disadvantage to itself, and the worker will continue in the company's employ despite possible advantage in moving to another firm.

2. Recruitment into the productive group is based on personal qualities without reference to a particular work task or set of skills. Selection is based primarily on the individual's education, character, and general background. Inadequacy or incompetence shown subsequent to selection are not a basis for dismissal from the group.

3. Status in the group is a continuation and extension of status held in the society at the time of entrance to the group. The broad dichotomy of employees into koin and shokuin limits the movement of an individual in the factory system largely to the general category that his education entitled him to enter on recruitment.

4. Reward in the productive group is only partly in the form of money, and is based on broad social criteria rather than on production criteria. The recompense of workers is made up of such items as housing, food, and personal services, with the actual cash pay of the worker forming only part of the total. Pay is based primarily on age, education, length of service, and family size, with job rank or competence only a small part of the criteria for determing work reward.

5. The formal organization of the factory is elaborated in a wide range and considerable number of formal positions. Formal rank and title in the hierarchy are well defined, but authority and responsibility of ranks are not. Partly in consequence, the decision-making

function is exercised by groups of persons, but responsibility for the decisions is not assigned to individuals.

6. The penetration of the company into the nonbusiness activities of the worker and the responsibility taken by the company for the worker are extensive. Management is involved in such diverse and intimate matters as the worker's personal finances, the education of his children, religious activities, and the training of the worker's wife. The company is responsible for the continued well-being of the worker and his family, and this responsibility is carried out both in formal personnel procedures and in the informal relations between the worker and supervisor.

If a single conclusion were to be drawn from this study it would be that the development of industrial Japan has taken place with much less change from the kinds of social organization and social relations of preindustrial or nonindustrial Japan than would be expected from the Western model of the growth of an industrial society. The rise and development of the industrial West is generally attributed in some considerable part to the development of an impersonalized and rationalized view of the world and of relations with others. Emphasis on individuality, the view of the workplace as a purely economic grouping clearly differentiated in goals and relationships from other areas of social interaction, the subordination of other values and interests of the economic goal in business activity, the use of money to discharge obligations for services in the business world—all these and related trends are seen as critical to the successful development of large-scale industry. In sociological theory some of these tendencies have been set forth in polarities to indicate the nature of the differences. Thus, for example, "status" and "contract" have been contrasted as indicating the difference and direction of development with industrialization from a close, intimate personal group to the more rationalized and impersonal-ized relations of modern business. A more recent dichotomization is the differentiation of "particularism" and "universalism," or the move from a value emphasis on particular relationships and symbols, with stress on loyalty and intragroup harmony, to an emphasis on rational-ized means-end relations, with stress on efficiency and performance.

These kinds of polarities are not altogether useful in discussing the Japanese case. Although it is possible to point to elements in the or-ganization of the Japanese factory that fit the industrial and modern end of these polarities, a very considerable part of the organizational system remains more like the preindustrial pole. It does not seem war-ranted to hold that Japan is now at some mid-point in development. Such an argument is inconsistent with the view that contractual, uni-versalistic relations are necessary to successful industrialization. Nor is it sufficient to say that since Japan's industrialization is relatively recent these divergencies from the pattern as seen and set forth in the West will in time mend themselves and fit harmoniously into one of these several categories without conflict or with few conflicting ele-ments. In point of fact, as this report has attempted to indicate, the Japanese system is on the whole self-consistent. The recruitment meth-ods and the incentive system fit together with the rules governing em-ployment to make a unified whole. Change in one, as, for example, in employment rules, would drastically affect and require changes in other elements of the organization.

From this examination of the Japanese factory, the factory organi-zation seems a consistent and logical outgrowth of the kinds of rela-tions existing in Japan prior to its industrialization. The changes that took place in Japan during the last three decades of the nineteenth century are often termed a "revolution." That they represented in many respects drastic departures from the preceding period is clear enough. The manner of the "revolution," however, seems still open to question. At repeated points in the study of the factory, parallels to an essentially feudal system of organization may be seen—not, to be sure, a replication of the feudal loyalties, commitments, rewards, and methods of leadership but a rephrasing of them in the setting of modern industry.

It may well be that the kinds of experiences undergone by the West antecedent to the development of modern industry are indeed essential to an independent and de novo development of industry. The Japanese case suggests that these experiences and the organizational system used in the West are not necessary to the introduction of industry into another social system. From the observations of this study it would appear that, although the technology of modern industry was introduced into Japan, the factory organization at the same time developed consistent with the historical customs and attitudes of the Japanese and with the social system as it existed prior to the introduction of modern industry. Thus, looking beyond the modern equipment and the formal organization, the systems of relationships are more nearly similar to those which seem to have characterized an earlier Japan and which now characterize the nonindustrial areas of Japan than they are similar to the factory organization of the West.

Differences in the role of the individual in the Western and Japanese factory—the ways in which he is motivated, the extent to which responsibility and authority are assigned individuals, the kinds of rewards offered, and the behaviors that are rewarded—have a close relation to differences between the two cultural backgrounds. Japan's

industry was superimposed in a matter of some few decades on a
society that was profoundly and had for some centuries been feudal.
The loyalty of the worker to the industrial organization, the paternal
methods of motivating and rewarding the worker, the close involvement
of the company in all manner of what seem to Western eyes to be personal and private affairs of the worker—all have parallels with Japan's
preindustrial social organization.

This parallel does not underestimate the enormous changes that have
taken place in Japan through the period of her industrialization. Japan
has changed mightily; and changes continue. If the study of industrialization in Japan is to be relevant to the study of the developing economies of other Asian nations, however, the nature of the changes
which have taken place must be clearly understood. What the results
of this study of the social organization of the large Japanese factory
suggest is that changes have taken place selectively—a point well remarked in other contexts—and, more important, that these changes
have been such as to leave unchanged the underlying basis of social
relationships. Rather than penetrating to the roots of the social system,
the changes have been built up from the kind of social relationships
pre-existing in Japan.

A compact statement of the general nature of social relations in
Japan has been provided by Stoetzel. He states: "In point of fact, as
Ruth Benedict rightly guessed, the whole social structure of Japan is
dictated by a concept of hierarchy deriving from the kinship of the
clan."[8] Stoetzel then summarizes his conclusions:

[8] Jean Stoetzel, Without the Chrysanthemum and the Sword: A Study of the
Attitudes of Youth in Postwar Japan, UNESCO publication (New York: Colum-
bia University Press, 1955), p. 56.

To understand the Japanese social structure, three ideas must be brought into play, not separately, but together: (a) the idea of kinship, by blood, marriage, adoption, or service; (b) the idea of hierarchy, always conceived more or less on the oyako (father-son) model; (c) the idea of sharing in the protection offered by the tutelary deities, by a common cult or at least by a common burying ground. These three ideas are connected with each other, particularly the first two: wherever there is kinship there is a hierarchical relationship, and the opposite as we have seen is also true; as for the common cult, it is the symbol of the family bond.[9]

Throughout this discussion of the large factory, parallels have been noted between the factory system and the clan or kinship organization. In terms of formal organization some of these have included both the manner of recruitment into the system and the kinds of reciprocal obligations thereby incurred by company and worker. Further, the formal system of motivation and reward has functional parallels to that of a kinship grouping.

In the informal organization as well the recurring relationship is modeled in the factory on the oyako relation, with hierarchical roles defined in terms of this pattern. This pattern is not, as pointed out earlier, the formal oyabun-kobun structure, but is, rather, an informal father-son type of system.

Indeed, so pervasive are the parallels to a kinship-type organization in the large Japanese factory that it is not necessary for the observer to argue their presence from indirect evidences. For example, in a 1952 speech to his managerial employees, the president of a large steel company said, "Not only is there the fact that our life's work is our employment in our company, but I feel that as people in this situation we have two occasions that can be called a 'birth.' The first is

[9] Ibid., p. 57.

when we are born into the world as mewling infants. The second is when we all receive our commissions of adoption into the company. This is an event that has the same importance as our crying birth." Here are both a direct statement of the kinship basis of company organization and an indication of the way in which the common bond is symbolized, by treating the company, its history, and present organization as an extended family with common values, common ancestors, and common beliefs. It is for this reason, for example, that elaborate histories and geneologies of the large firms are written and that common religious shrines and ceremonies may be found.

It might be added here parenthetically and as a further evidence of the nature of these underlying relationships that the zaibatsu groupings in Japan are seriously misunderstood when seen as cartels or monopolies on the Western model. These are in a very real sense clans, the furthest extension of kinship-type relations in the economic and industrial sector. To treat these, by the passing of anti-monopoly laws, as fundamentally economic and financial groupings was grotesque and doomed to failure from the first. It might be pertinent here to quote Lockwood again: "Too often in the case of Japan there is a tendency to apply easy labels, derived from Western experience. They may only obscure the complexities of the facts."[10] This statement does not say that the factory organization is "caused" by Japanese family organization but that both family organization and factory organization are components of a common social structure; and as such the system of relationships within each grouping has a common structural base.

It would seem from this study, then, that the very success of the Japanese experience with industrialization may well have been a

[10]Lockwood, op. cit., p. 200.

function of the fact that, far from undergoing a total revolution in social structure or social relationships, the hard core of Japan's system of social relationships remained intact, allowing an orderly transition to industrialization continuous with her earlier social forms. It would in fact be remarkable if social change of this magnitude and success could occur in any other way. Discontinuity will not lead to effective adaptation; rather, it will result in chaos. The exceptional durability of Japan's social system, often remarked upon and demonstrated anew in her response to total defeat in the Second World War, is not the result of a mystic ability of the Japanese to adapt but, rather, the consequence of the fact that through change a basis for social continuity has remained intact. It is of some interest to note in this connection that the same wondrous ability to selectively take on new elements in a society is now being attributed to Indian society. But selective adaptation should not be remarkable; it would be much more remarkable if any people were able in one fell swoop to put off their past, their training, and habits of mind and don successfully and permanently totally new social paraphernalia. Efforts to change the economy of other nations in the direction of industrialization might better then be concerned with an identification of basic elements of the preindustrial social system and with the introduction of new technologies and financial systems in the context of the older relationships, than with making these nations over in the image derived from Western outcomes.

A partial explanation, therefore, of Japan's rapid industrialization might well be argued to lie in the amount and more especially in the kind of continuity throughout the transition rather than in an emphasis on change. In this connection one might note that there is reason to believe that the pressure of the family system in Japan toward social rigidity and inflexibility may be commonly overstated. Although an analysis of the family system is outside the limits of this study, in terms of the thesis of social continuity and its effects on industrial change, it should be emphasized that in two particulars at least there has been within the historical structure of the Japanese family a potentiality for flexibility and change.

The first of these is the practice of adoption, by which not only more distant relatives but also able and promising employees and servants have long been able to assume important roles in higher-status families and in family businesses. This practice, not far removed from the notion of employment as seen in the large factory, not only has made for continual social mobility and flexibility even under feudal regulations but also may well have provided a paradigm for methods of industrial recruitment.

The role of the younger son in Japan is also of some interest in this regard. Under rules of primogeniture in a country lacking sufficient land there are provided the conditions for the establishment of an urban work force. Further, there has been a tradition of continuity, despite such mobility by younger sons, through the establishment of "branch families" tied to the "main family" by bonds of obligation and duty. The main family, in, for example, a rural village, under industrialization also provided a buffer against economic hardship and depression—an advantage still in a country where social security measures are meager.

These and other elements of the Japanese family structure, aspects of family organization conducive to adaptation and change, may well have aided the transition to industrialization by making possible adjustment within the older family system rather than, as is sometimes suggested, industrialization and urbanization shattering the older family pattern. Finally, and most important from the point of view of factory organization, the principle of family loyalty and cohesion, when successfully symbolized and incorporated into military, industrial, and financial organizations, may have become an important source of energy and motivation for the transition to industrialization. It must again be emphasized that such structural elements as these would hold change within limits, order the great transition, and prevent the kind of social discontinuity which would be destructive of a society.

Turning now from such suggestions as this study of the large Japanese factory might provide for an understanding of Japan's past, we raise the question of possible future developments in the organization of Japanese industry. There is a perhaps inherent tendency in describing an on-going social organization to emphasize the integration and harmony of the several elements of the system at the expense of an analysis of stress or of present and future changes in the system. Yet in reviewing the Japanese factory the system appears to be stable in terms of the relationships between people in the organization. The organization is internally consistent and acceptable to its members so long as the membership is drawn from backgrounds in which the forms of relationships on which the factory is based are retained.

In terms of the people in the factory, two groups in particular seem to have some difficulty in adapting themselves to this kind of organization. Young Japanese who are urban reared, born in the large cities of laboring and white collar fathers, educated in urban schools beyond the legally prescribed minimum of middle school education, and steeped in the impersonality of modern cities do not fit well into these factory relationships. Here is a central problem of the large Japanese factory. Workers born into traditional extended and close-knit families in the farm villages of Japan, for example, have, in the words of the factory managers, "stable natures." Products of small family groups of the large cities, unfamiliar with the elaborate systems of obligations and duties spun by kinship and friendship ties in the stable villages, do not respond to the appeals and rationale of this factory system. Women, too, who by virtue of family training or education have been schooled in a newer pattern of relationships and role expectations and who have come to expect an occupational role different from that traditionally assigned Japanese women, protest their position in the factory.

Changes in the factory organization may proceed from two causes. The first is prior changes in the organization of and relationships in primary groups in the society. The second is the pressure of changes in technology and production methods that would lead to organizational change. The demands of technology and output have been discussed in the preceding chapter on productivity. The pressure for change is great, for example, to increase the flexibility of the work force to lead to greater adaptability to economic changes. The need for change has led, on occasion, to change in a limited sphere, as, for example, when a financial crisis and a subsequent "rationalization" movement led to the discharge of employees from a number of large factories. As in the case described in Chapter 2, however, it appears likely that makeshift and temporary adaptations which do not alter the general rules of employ-ment and organization will be made. Real changes in factory organiza-tion will come about only when the point of view and the training of individuals in the system alter significantly. Thus the Japanese family system, under the pressure of urbanization, changes in religious thought and training, and under the constant impact of mass communication, may change the ways in which youths are trained and developed, thus changing the attitudes and expectations, motivation systems, and inter-action patterns of youth. Although changes in primary group structures have not yet been carried to the point where the factory organization is in conflict with any major portion of the society's patterns of inter- action, such a process of change, in large part the result of the growth of large industry, may in time alter the basis of factory organization.

It is easy here, as In looking at Japanese history, to mistake the nature of changes in cities and during the postwar period. The general formulas for the effects of urbanization have been developed out of Western experience. The almost total lack of close study of the nature of social interaction in the cities of Asia makes a prediction of the di- rection and kind of change induced by urbanization in Asia most haz- ardous. Further, it is far from clear at present as to how effective and lasting postwar experiments and adjustments may be in the Japanese case. It would be a daring observer indeed who would predict the out- come of the next two or three decades of Japanese events.

In summing up the results of this study, there appear to be two broad elements of difference between Japan and the West in relation to the nature of the social organization of the factory. First, the factory, or company, is relatively undifferentiated from other types of groups in the society. In terms of the commitment of members to the group, the nature of their recruitment and subsequent careers, and the extent of involvement of members with each other as part of the group, the Japa- nese factory grouping parallels other social groupings. Although the factory may be defined as an economic organization with its goals narrowly defined and relationships narrowly based on productivity and profit, the Japanese factory is not so defined. The Western view of life segments, each serving a special end with differentiated relation- ships in each—the family, the club or association, the workplace—makes possible a clear differentiation of activities and organization in each group. In Japan, the factory recruits involve and maintain their membership on a basis similar to that of the domestic and social groups of the society. Where the economic ends of the factory conflict with this broader definition of the group, as in the case of the incompetent employee who will not be discharged, the economic ends take a secondary position to the maintenance of group integrity.

This lack of differentiation between the large factory organization and other social groupings is not only an internal one. Status in the broader community, as reflected primarily in educational attainment, is the critical variable governing recruitment and is the dominating factor in rank and career progress in the factory. Moreover, the employee shares responsibility with the company for his family, his children, and his general well-being. The broader social activities are not set apart from his membership in the factory or company.

Closely related to this latter aspect of the lack of differentiation is the difference between the American and the Japanese organization in the extent to which there is an individualization or impersonalization of relationships in the factory. It is perhaps this lack of individualization that most sets off the day-to-day functioning of the Japanese production unit from its American counterpart. The apparatus of modern production in the West depends heavily on the assignment of individual responsibility, on individual incentive programs, on the job evaluation of the individual employee, and on a system of rewards in which individual competence and energy will be recompensed. In all of these respects the difference from Japan is marked. Individual responsibility is avoided, incentive systems have little relationship to individual output but, rather, depend on group success, and the motivating of energies appears to depend on the individuals's loyalty and identification with the group and with his superior.

In short, it may be concluded from this study that, although the pre-industrial experience of the West may indeed have been the necessary cause of the development of industrialization, the introduction of industry into a society like that of Japan, which has not shared these earlier experiences and has a markedly different social system, makes necessary the fitting of the industrial mechanism to the earlier social system. What must also be noted is the considerable industrial success that is possible under these circumstances. It may be true that the Western style of organization maximizes productivity, but substantial industrial progress can be made within quite a different style of organization. Rationalization and impersonalization are not, the Japanese experience seems to argue, necessary to the adoption from the West of an industrial economy.

That the amalgam of a preindustrial system of organization and Western technology has created problems for Japanese industry is very clear, and some of the problems have been stressed in this report. It does not follow from the fact that problems exist that their solution lies in the direction of greater change toward the Western business model. This might be the case in some areas, as, for example, in terms of problems of sales and distribution where Western methods need not disrupt upon their introduction the on-going organizational system. When other Western elements are introduced, however, whether by Western or Japanese advisors, the outcomes will often not be so harmless. Such introductions of new and Western techniques and approaches must be considered with some caution by American experts and consultants.

More relevant perhaps to present concerns of the United States are the possible implications of the Japanese experience in the problem of aiding the development of other non-Western nations. It would seem

from the Japanese example that a considerable degree of tolerance—
even at the cost of seeming waste—needs to be allowed local custom
and methods in establishing industry in those countries with systems of
interpersonal relations markedly different from those of the West.   A
lasting and effective transition to industrialization may be accomplished
only when the changes are continuous with the preindustrial social system and are based on and grow out of the patterns of social interaction
basic to the society.

PERENNIAL WORKS IN SOCIOLOGY

An Arno Press Collection

Abegglen, James [C.] **The Japanese Factory: Aspects of Its Social Organization.** 1958

Aron, Raymond. **German Sociology.** Translated by Mary and Thomas Bottomore. 1964

Bernard, L[uther] L[ee.] **Instinct: A Study in Social Psychology.** 1924

Chapin, F. Stuart. **Field Work and Social Research.** 1920

Coleman, James S., et at. **Equality of Educational Opportunity.** 1966

DeGré, Gerard. **Society and Ideology: An Inquiry Into the Sociology of Knowledge.** 1943

Granick, David. **The European Executive.** 1962

Granick, David. **The Red Executive: A Study of the Organization Man in Russian Industry.** 1960

Hughes, Everett Cherrington. **The Chicago Real Estate Board: The Growth of an Institution.** 1931

Keller, Suzanne. **Beyond the Ruling Class: Strategic Elites in Modern Society.** 1963

Lazarsfeld, Paul F. and Patricia L. Kendall. **Radio Listening in America: The People Look at Radio—Again.** 1948

Lazarsfeld, Paul F. and Frank Stanton, eds. **Communications Research, 1948-1949.** 1949

Lazarsfeld, Paul F. and Frank N. Stanton, eds. **Radio Research, 1941.** 1941

Lazarsfeld, Paul F. and Frank N. Stanton, eds. **Radio Research, 1942-1943.** 1944

Lévy-Bruhl, Lucien. **How Natives Think.** Translated by Lilian A. Clare. 1926

Pareto, Volfredo. **The Rise and Fall of the Elites: An Application of Theoretical Sociology.** Introduction by Hans L. Zetterberg. 1968

President's Research Committee on Social Trends. **Recent Social Trends in the United States, Volumes I and II.** With a Foreward by Herbert Hoover. 1933

Powdermaker, Hortense. **Hollywood: The Dream Factory; An Anthropologist Looks at the Movie-Makers.** 1950

Rainwater, Lee, Richard P. Coleman and Gerald Handel. **Workingman's Wife: Her Personality, World and Life Style.** Preface by W. Lloyd Warner; Introduction by Burleigh B. Gardner. 1959

Riesman, David, in collaboration with Nathan Glazer. **Faces in the Crowd: Individual Studies in Character and Politics.** 1952

Rogoff, Natalie. **Recent Trends in Occupational Mobility.** With a Foreword by Herbert Goldhamer. 1953

Rosenberg, Bernard and Norris Fliegel. **The Vanguard Artist: Portrait and Self-Portrait.** 1965

Roth, Guenther. **The Social Democrats in Imperial Germany: A Study in Working-Class Isolation and National Integration.** Preface by Reinhard Bendix. 1963

Selznick, Philip. **The Organizational Weapon: A Study of Bolshevik Strategy and Tactics.** 1960

Simmel, Georg. **Sociology of Religion.** Translated from the German by Curt Rosenthal. [1959]

Sorokin, Pitirim A. **Sociological Theories of Today.** 1966

Sumner, William Graham. **Folkways: A Study of the Sociological Importance of Usages, Manners, Customs, Mores, and Morals.** With a Special Introduction by William Lyon Phelps. 1940

Svalastoga, Kaare. **Prestige, Class and Mobility.** 1959

Tiryakian, Edward A. **Sociologism and Existentialism: Two Perspectives on the Individual and Society.** 1962

Walker, Charles, R. and Robert H. Guest. **The Man on the Assembly Line.** 1952

Warner, W. Lloyd and James C. Abegglen. **Occupational Mobility in American Business and Industry, 1928-1952.** 1955

Wilson, Robert N., ed. **The Arts in Society.** 1964

Wolff, Kurt H., ed. **Emile Durkheim, 1858-1917: A Collection of Essays, with Translations and a Bibliography.** 1960

Wood, Robert C. **Suburbia: Its People and Their Politics.** 1959 face.